# The Sleepiest Bedtime Stories for Kids 5 to 10

## A COLLECTION OF RELAXING TALES TO HELP YOUR KIDS FALL ASLEEP FAST

WILLOW WIGGINS

GO PUBLISHING LLC

# Contents

# Introduction

Hello there, friend! My name is Willow Wiggins, and I'm so excited that you're joining me on this cozy journey of bedtime stories. I've always had a love for children's books—there's something magical about stories that can whisk you off to enchanted places just before drifting into a peaceful sleep. I have two little ones of my own, and every night, reading them a story or two is one of my favorite parts of the day. Those quiet moments, cuddled up together, watching their eyes grow heavy as they drift into dreamland, fill my heart with joy.

As my kids grew, I noticed how they loved stories that felt like little adventures but still brought a sense of calm. They wanted tales that made them smile and imagine yet left them feeling safe and ready for bed. So,

I began crafting these bedtime stories for them, creating little worlds that sparkled with gentle magic, friendly creatures, and endless wonder. I found myself inventing characters like the kind-hearted Star Carvers who sculpt stars from clouds or the curious children who discover hidden places like the Starlight Library. Each story opened a soft, comforting world where my children could feel wrapped up in warmth and peace.

Over time, I realized these stories could help more than just my own little ones. They became my way of offering children everywhere a way to gently say goodbye to the day and embrace sleep with excitement, calm, and curiosity. Each of these stories has a special magic—a way of encouraging a gentle sigh, a deep breath, and a smile as little ones close their eyes and drift away. After all, bedtime should be something to look forward to, not just the end of a day but the beginning of a journey into dreams.

As you read these stories to your own children (or play them if you're listening to the audiobook), I hope you'll find moments of joy, surprise, and coziness. Maybe you'll even discover a few favorites that will be requested over and over, the ones that become part of your nighttime routine like an old, comforting friend. And who knows? Perhaps these stories will even inspire dreams of star-filled skies, friendly woodland creatures, or magical places hidden just out of sight.

So, welcome to our collection of "Sleepiest Bedtime Stories." These tales are for every child who loves a little bit of magic before bed, for every parent who cherishes that last story of the night, and for anyone who believes that dreams are just as important as the adventures we have during the day.

Find a cozy spot, snuggle in, and let the magic of these stories carry you gently into slumber. Sweet dreams are waiting just around the corner. And who knows what wonderful places you might discover tonight?

# The Dreamy Balloon Ride

In the peaceful little town of Moonville, bedtime was the most magical time of day. While other towns simply grew quiet under the night sky, Moonville seemed to glow with a special kind of light, like it had its own secret world hidden above. Every child in Moonville had heard whispers of a mysterious balloon that appeared only when the stars were especially bright—a balloon that could take you all the way to the clouds.

Seven-year-old Milo had heard the story a hundred times. He loved the idea of a dreamy balloon that would float you up to the stars, to places you could only imagine. So, every night, after he brushed his teeth and climbed under his cozy quilt, he'd gaze out his window and make a wish. "Maybe tonight," he'd whisper, watching the stars twinkle in the dark sky.

One cool, quiet evening, after a long day of playing in the garden and chasing butterflies, Milo nestled into bed, feeling extra sleepy. As he drifted off, he heard a soft, gentle tapping at his window. His eyes fluttered open, and there it was—a glowing, golden balloon hovering just outside, casting a warm light into his room.

With a sleepy but delighted smile, Milo tiptoed to the window and opened it wide. The balloon had a big, cozy basket attached, and it seemed to be waiting just for him. He climbed in, his heart beating fast with excitement, and as soon as he was settled, the balloon floated up as softly as a feather on a breeze.

As they rose above Moonville, Milo looked down to see the little houses and treetops growing smaller and smaller. The town lights looked like twinkling stars scattered across the ground. "Wow," Milo whispered, feeling as if he were a tiny bird soaring over a glittering village.

Just then, a soft, giggling sound filled the air. Milo turned and saw a small, puffy creature floating beside him. It looked like a cloud, with a gentle, shimmering glow, round cheeks, and eyes that sparkled like the night sky.

"Hello, Milo!" the cloud creature chirped in a voice as soft as a lullaby. "My name is Daisy, and I'll be your guide through the night sky."

Milo's eyes widened with excitement. "Hello, Daisy! Are we really going up to the clouds?"

"Oh, much further than that," Daisy replied with a grin. "We're going on a tour of the whole night sky!"

The balloon rose higher, drifting toward the stars. Milo felt like he was floating in a dream, and Daisy pointed out constellations as they glided along. "Look over there," she said, pointing to a cluster of stars that formed the shape of a bear. "That's Ursa Major, the Great Bear. He watches over the night, making sure all the stars are in their places."

Milo gazed at the stars, feeling a calm warmth inside him. "Does the bear ever sleep?" he asked.

Daisy chuckled softly. "Oh, he takes little naps during the day when the sun's out. But at night, he's busy watching over everyone like a big, sleepy guardian."

As they drifted further, Milo spotted a river of shimmering light that seemed to flow across the sky like a river. "What's that?" he asked, pointing.

"That's the Milky Way," Daisy said. "It's a special river made of stardust. When a star finishes its time shining in the sky, it drifts down to the Milky Way and becomes part of the Stardust River. Sometimes, if you're very quiet, you can hear it humming a gentle song."

Milo closed his eyes for a moment, listening to the faint hum. It sounded like a soft lullaby, and it made him feel peaceful, as if the entire universe was singing him to sleep.

Just then, they floated past a tall, old tree with wide branches. Perched in the branches were three owls, each wearing tiny, round glasses and gazing up at the stars. They turned to look at Milo and Daisy, blinking their wise, sleepy eyes.

"Good evening, young Milo," one of the owls hooted softly. "We are the Stargazing Owls. Every night, we watch the stars and whisper their stories to each other."

"Would you like to hear a story, Milo?" asked the second owl, her voice gentle and slow.

Milo nodded eagerly. "Yes, please!"

The third owl, with feathers as white as snow, leaned in close and began to speak in a low, soothing voice. "Once upon a time, in a galaxy far, far away, there was a brave little star named Nova. Nova wanted to shine brighter than any other star, so she traveled to the very edge of the universe, gathering all the light she could find. And every time a new star looks a little brighter, we know that Nova has shared her light with them."

Milo's eyelids grew heavy as he listened, feeling as if Nova's light was filling him with warmth. The owls waved goodbye as Daisy guided the balloon higher, where they found a sky dotted with colorful planets. Each planet glowed softly, some red, some blue, and some shimmering in shades of purple and green.

"Those are the Dream Planets," Daisy explained. "Each one holds a different kind of dream, like dreams of flying or dreams of exploring magical forests. Every night, children all over the world visit the Dream Planets when they close their eyes and drift to sleep."

"Can we visit one?" Milo asked with a sleepy grin.

Daisy smiled, her twinkling eyes warm and kind. "Oh, we're already visiting. This balloon ride is a special dream, just for you."

Milo felt his heart fill with joy and peace. He looked down at the twinkling town below, then back up at the starlit sky above. Everything seemed perfect, as if he was right where he was meant to be. A shooting star zipped by, leaving a trail of glittering light behind it.

"Make a wish, Milo!" Daisy whispered.

Closing his eyes, Milo made a wish, thinking of all the wonderful things he'd seen—the stargazing owls, the Dream Planets, the glowing river of stardust. He wished to always remember this magical night, to keep it in his heart like a cozy blanket he could snuggle into whenever he needed it.

As he opened his eyes, he felt the balloon begin to drift down, soft and slow, like a feather falling from the sky. The stars twinkled goodbye, and the planets glowed a little brighter as if they were all waving him off.

Daisy hummed a soft tune, the same lullaby he'd heard in the Milky Way, and Milo's eyes grew heavier and heavier. As the balloon gently touched down outside his window, Milo stepped out, feeling drowsy but so happy. He gave Daisy a hug, and she wrapped her soft, cloud-like arms around him.

"Goodnight, Milo," she whispered. "Remember, the stars are always watching over you."

Milo climbed back into his bed, pulling his cozy quilt up to his chin. As he drifted off to sleep, he felt the warmth of the stars, the hum of the Milky Way, and the soft lullaby of the night sky surrounding him. And just as his eyes closed, he saw Daisy give one last glowing wave, floating away into the starry night.

With a peaceful smile, Milo sank into the deepest, coziest sleep he'd ever known, dreaming of more adventures under the twinkling sky.

# Luna's Secret Garden

In the quiet village of Willowbrook, there lived a kind-hearted little girl named Luna. Luna had a gentle spirit and a deep love for flowers and nature. Every night before bed, she would tend to the window-box garden outside her bedroom. She had planted a few flowers there—delicate daisies, tiny lavender buds, and one tall sunflower that stretched as far as it could toward the sky. Luna would water each plant, whisper goodnight to them, and then watch as their leaves seemed to glisten under the soft glow of the moonlight.

One particular evening, Luna had spent extra time with her garden. She had whispered special wishes for each plant, wishing for them to grow strong, bright, and happy. Just as she was about to turn away, something caught her eye. There, beneath her window box, was a single, sparkling flower petal, shimmering as if it were dusted with tiny stars.

Curious, Luna bent down to look at it. The petal was a deep blue, with tiny sparkles that glowed softly, like moonlight trapped in a single leaf. She looked around, wondering where it had come from. Then she noticed something even more peculiar—a trail of these glowing petals, each one leading gently toward the backyard.

*Where could these petals lead?* Luna wondered, her heart fluttering with excitement and curiosity.

Without a second thought, Luna followed the trail, tiptoeing through her backyard under the starlit sky. Each petal seemed to light up the ground beneath her, creating a path that glimmered like a trail of stars. She felt as though she were walking in a dream, her bare feet pressing into the cool grass, the soft night breeze whispering secrets in her ear.

The trail led her to the very back of the garden, to a place she had rarely ventured. Here, hidden beneath a blanket of ivy, was a small wooden gate she'd never noticed before. It looked old, with a faded design of swirling vines carved into the wood, as if it had been waiting just for her.

With a small push, Luna opened the gate, and it creaked softly as if it were sighing after a long rest.

Beyond the gate lay a secret garden, glowing under the soft light of the full moon. Luna gasped, her eyes widening with wonder. The garden was like nothing she'd ever seen before.

Enormous flowers taller than her stood in shades of pink, blue, and lavender, their petals glowing with a gentle, magical light. Delicate mushrooms dotted the ground, each shimmering with its own faint glow, like tiny lanterns lighting up the path. The trees hummed a soft lullaby, their leaves rustling in a gentle rhythm as if they, too, were singing along.

Luna walked into the garden, her heart filled with awe. She noticed small, twinkling lights flitting between the flowers and trees and realized they were tiny fireflies, casting a warm, golden glow that danced across the leaves.

As she explored, she heard a soft giggle, like the sound of chimes in the breeze. Turning around, Luna saw a small figure hovering beside a giant sunflower. It was a tiny, winged creature with delicate, translucent wings that glowed like starlight. She had wild hair as green as grass, and her dress was made of petals and leaves.

"Hello, Luna!" the creature said, her voice warm and cheerful. "I've been waiting for you. My name is

Thistle. I'm a garden fairy and the keeper of this Secret Garden."

Luna's eyes sparkled with delight. "Hello, Thistle! This garden is the most beautiful place I've ever seen."

Thistle smiled, her eyes twinkling. "Thank you! It's a very special garden, but tonight, it's a little restless. The garden creatures can't seem to settle down, and they're keeping each other awake. Could you help me calm them so they can get a good night's sleep?"

Luna nodded eagerly. "I'd love to help."

Thistle led Luna through the garden, guiding her toward a patch of flowers with sleepy, half-closed petals. "These flowers need to be lulled to sleep," Thistle explained. "They close their petals when they feel calm and cozy, but tonight, they're a bit too excited."

Luna leaned close to the flowers, gently brushing her fingers over their soft petals. She began to hum a lullaby, just like her mother would hum to her every night before bed. As she hummed, she noticed the flowers slowly closing their petals as if they were drifting off to sleep. Thistle sprinkled a handful of soft, sparkling moon dust over them, and the flowers let out a contented sigh, settling into a peaceful slumber.

"Lovely work, Luna!" Thistle praised, her voice as soft as a whisper. "Now, let's help the ladybugs."

They continued walking until they found a cluster of ladybugs perched on a large leaf. The little creatures were fidgeting and shuffling, their tiny legs scurrying back and forth. "These ladybugs are so tired, but they've had a busy night exploring and can't seem to calm down," Thistle explained.

Luna reached out, her touch gentle and light, and whispered softly to each ladybug. "It's time for sleep, little friends," she said. "Close your eyes and rest."

Thistle sprinkled moon dust over the ladybugs, and one by one, they settled into tiny grooves in the leaf, their bodies still and peaceful. Luna smiled, feeling warmth in her heart as she watched them fall asleep, their red shells glowing softly in the moonlight.

Just as they were finishing with the ladybugs, a gust of wind rustled through the garden, making the leaves shiver and dance. The branches swayed, their hum turning from a gentle lullaby into a restless tune.

"Oh dear," Thistle said, her brow furrowing. "The wind is keeping the trees awake, and it's making them too restless to sleep."

Luna looked around and saw the leaves shaking and quivering as if they were chattering among themselves. She placed her hand on the trunk of the nearest tree, feeling its cool, sturdy bark under her fingertips.

"Shh," Luna whispered, calming her voice. "It's all right. Let's all take a deep breath."

She breathed in slowly, and as if they could sense her calmness, the trees began to slow their swaying. Thistle sprinkled moon dust over the branches, and the trees responded with a gentle sigh, their hum returning to a soft, soothing lullaby.

As they moved through the garden, Luna and Thistle helped all the garden creatures settle down. They visited clusters of sleepy moths, brushing their wings with moon dust until they lay still, like tiny silk blankets scattered on the leaves. They sang to the drowsy butterflies, who tucked themselves under petals, resting their wings.

Finally, Luna noticed a small patch of shimmering bluebells that seemed to be humming along with the trees. She knelt beside them, touching each delicate petal. "Goodnight, little bluebells," she whispered, her voice gentle and warm.

Thistle joined her, her tiny wings fluttering softly as she sprinkled one last handful of moon dust over the flowers. "Now the garden can sleep," she whispered, a look of contentment on her face.

Luna looked around, seeing the garden completely at peace. The flowers were tucked in, their petals closed, the trees swayed gently with the softest breeze, and all the creatures were nestled and still, wrapped in the calm of the moonlight.

Thistle turned to Luna, her eyes shining with gratitude. "Thank you, Luna. You've brought peace to the garden tonight."

"It was wonderful," Luna replied, her own heart feeling warm and full. She felt her own eyes growing heavy as if the peace of the garden were settling over her, too. "I wish I could stay here forever."

Thistle smiled and reached up, plucking a single flower from a nearby bush. It glowed with a soft light, a gentle blue that reminded Luna of starlight. "Take this," Thistle said, placing the glowing flower in Luna's hand. "It's a piece of the garden's magic to keep with you wherever you go. Just look at it, and you'll always feel the peace of this place."

Luna held the flower close, feeling its warmth spread through her fingers. "Thank you, Thistle. I'll treasure it."

Thistle gave her a gentle hug, her tiny arms wrapping around Luna's fingers. "Goodnight, Luna. The garden will always be here, waiting for you."

With a final wave, Luna made her way back to the wooden gate. She stepped through, and as she turned to look back, she saw the garden glowing softly under the moonlight, peaceful and still. She closed the gate, feeling a calmness settle over her, and made her way back through the sparkling petal trail that led to her window.

When Luna climbed back into her room, she placed the glowing flower on her bedside table. Its soft light filled her room, casting gentle shadows that danced along the walls. She climbed into bed, pulling her blanket up to her chin, and closed her eyes, feeling the warmth of the secret garden still in her heart.

As she drifted off to sleep, she could almost hear the soft hum of the trees, the whisper of the flowers, and the gentle lullaby of the garden creatures, all singing her into the deepest, most peaceful sleep she'd ever known.

And as she dreamed, Luna knew that the secret garden was waiting for her, just beyond the gate, a world of magic and peace under the light of the moon.

# Finn and The Wishing Star Pond

Finn was a thoughtful boy with a wild imagination, and he spent his days dreaming of all the magical places he hoped to visit someday. Every morning, he would look up at the sky and wonder what it would be like to float among the stars or maybe even find a hidden world that no one else had ever seen. His mind was a treasure chest full of wishes, each one a small spark waiting for the perfect moment to come to life.

One summer evening, Finn and his family went on a camping trip deep into the forest. They set up their tent near a meadow, surrounded by tall trees that seemed to stretch up to the sky, their leaves whispering in the evening breeze. Finn loved the forest—it was quiet yet alive with the sounds of crickets, rustling leaves, and the distant hoot of an owl. But as much as he enjoyed exploring, he was also a little disappointed. It was hard to make wishes out here in the woods, with no stars visible through the thick canopy of trees.

As the sun dipped lower and the shadows grew longer, Finn's grandmother noticed his wandering gaze and gave him a gentle smile. She was a kind, wise woman who always seemed to know what he was thinking. "Finn," she said softly, "do you know about the Wishing Star Pond?"

Finn's eyes lit up. "No, Grandma. What's the Wishing Star Pond?"

His grandma leaned closer, her eyes twinkling with the same light he imagined the stars might have. "The Wishing Star Pond is a secret place hidden deep within the forest. It only reveals itself to those who truly believe in the magic of wishes. When the night is quiet and the stars are bright, the pond reflects the light of every star in the sky. And if you're lucky enough to find it, you're granted one special wish."

Finn's heart raced. "Do you think I could find it?"

His grandma chuckled and patted his hand. "If anyone could, it's you, my dear."

With that, she gave him a small flashlight and kissed him on the forehead. "Follow the path of fireflies," she whispered, "and keep your heart open to wonder."

Finn took a deep breath and set off down the path, excitement bubbling up inside him. As he walked, tiny fireflies appeared one by one, lighting the way with their gentle, golden glow. They flitted along the trees, guiding him deeper into the forest. The further he went, the quieter the woods became, as if every creature were waiting for something special to happen.

Finally, he reached a small clearing, and there it was —the Wishing Star Pond. The pond was small but perfectly round, like a silver mirror resting in the earth. Its surface shimmered with the light of a thousand stars, reflecting the night sky as if the heavens themselves had come down to rest on its waters. Finn felt his heart swell with awe and wonder. The sight was so beautiful, so magical, that he almost forgot to breathe.

He knelt by the edge of the pond, peering into its depths. He could see each star shining brightly, a perfect reflection of the sky above. The stars seemed to twinkle just for him, casting gentle glimmers of light that danced across his face. Finn remembered his grandmother's words—he could make one special wish.

Taking a deep breath, he closed his eyes and whispered his wish, a wish he had held in his heart for as long as he could remember. He wished for peaceful dreams filled with wonder and magic, dreams that would take him to places beyond his imagination. It was a simple wish but one that filled him with a sense of calm and joy.

When he opened his eyes, he lay down on the soft grass beside the pond, gazing up at the twinkling sky. As he watched, something extraordinary happened. The stars above began to shimmer even brighter, their light casting a soft, warm glow over him. He felt as though the universe itself was watching over him, embracing him with a peaceful calm.

Then, a gentle, melodic whisper filled the air, a sound so soft he almost thought he was dreaming. "Hello, Finn," the stars seemed to say, their voices blending together like a lullaby. "Would you like to hear some of our stories?"

Finn's eyes grew wide with delight. "Yes, please," he whispered, his voice full of wonder.

The stars began to share tales of far-off galaxies and hidden worlds, stories of places Finn could barely imagine. They spoke of shimmering nebulas where colors danced and swirled, creating vast paintings across the sky. They told him of sleepy space whales that drifted through the cosmos, their songs echoing through the universe like the soft hum of a lullaby.

One star, a small twinkling one that shone just a bit brighter, told him a story about a comet named

Blaze who loved to zoom through the sky at incredible speeds. Every night, Blaze would rush past the planets, circling the stars before saying a gentle "goodnight" and disappearing into the dark. Finn could almost picture the comet's trail, like a streak of silver fire lighting up the night.

The stars told him about twinkling starfish that lived in the ocean of a distant planet. These starfish would gather each night on the shore, waiting for the moon to rise and fill the sky with light. When the moon's glow touched the water, the starfish would glow in return, creating a sea of sparkling lights that stretched as far as the eye could see.

Finn listened, captivated, his mind drifting with each gentle story. He felt as though he were floating, traveling to each far-off place, guided by the whispers of the stars. The stories filled him with a warm, peaceful feeling as if he were wrapped in a cozy blanket of stardust.

As he lay there, the stars continued to hum softly, sharing more tales of the universe's mysteries. They told him about the Timekeeper Owl, an ancient owl who lived on the moon and watched over the passage of time. Every night, the Timekeeper Owl would look down on the world, making sure each second and minute slipped by as it should. The stars said that if you listened closely enough, you could hear the owl's quiet hoot, marking the rhythm of the night.

Finn closed his eyes, his imagination swirling with images of sleepy space creatures, glowing starfish, and the wise Timekeeper Owl. He felt a deep sense of calm settle over him, a peace that seemed to flow from the stars and into his heart. It was as if the whole universe had stopped for a moment just to share these stories with him, and he felt grateful for each and every one.

He lay there for what felt like hours, though time seemed to have slowed, the minutes stretching like soft, silken threads. The stars continued to hum their lullabies, filling the air with a sense of timeless peace. Finn's wish was coming true; he felt the peaceful dreams already beginning to take shape in his mind, each one more magical than the last.

Just as his eyes grew heavy, the stars whispered one final story, a gentle tale about the Wishing Star Pond itself. The pond, they said, was as old as the forest and had been hidden there for centuries, waiting for children with open hearts and big dreams. Each child who found the pond could make a wish, and the pond would share its peace with them, filling their dreams with the quiet magic of the night.

With a contented sigh, Finn let his eyes close, feeling the warmth of the stars on his skin, like tiny kisses from the universe. The last thing he saw before drifting into sleep was the soft shimmer of the Wishing Star Pond, glowing like a mirror of the night sky.

As he slept, Finn dreamed of all the magical places the stars had shown him. He floated among galaxies painted with colors he'd never seen, drifted alongside the sleepy space whales, and watched Blaze the comet race across the sky, leaving trails of silver light. He visited the distant planet with the twinkling starfish and listened to the hoot of the Timekeeper Owl as it watched over the passage of time.

In his dream, he felt a soft hand on his shoulder, and he turned to see his grandmother, her face filled with warmth and love. She smiled at him, her eyes twinkling like the stars, and whispered, "Sweet dreams, my dear Finn. The stars are watching over you."

When Finn finally woke, the first rays of dawn were peeking over the trees, casting a gentle light over the forest. The Wishing Star Pond still shimmered beside him, though its glow was softer now, like the fading memory of a dream. He sat up, feeling rested and peaceful as if the magic of the night had wrapped itself around him like a blanket.

As he made his way back to the campsite, his heart was full of gratitude and wonder. He knew he would never forget the stories the stars had shared, and he felt a quiet happiness knowing that the Wishing Star Pond would always be there, waiting for him.

That morning, as he told his grandmother about his adventure, she listened with a knowing smile. When he finished, she gave him a hug, her arms warm and comforting. "The Wishing Star Pond is a special place," she said softly. "It only reveals itself to those who believe in magic and who hold their wishes close to their hearts."

Finn smiled, feeling as if he'd been let in on a wonderful secret. That night, as he lay in his tent, he looked up through the small opening above him and whispered a quiet thank you to the stars. They twinkled back at him as if to say, *You're welcome.*

As he drifted into sleep, he felt the peaceful presence of the Wishing Star Pond in his heart, knowing that the world was filled with magic and wonder, and he could visit it each night. What a joy!

# The Sleepy River Voyage

In a cozy little village, right at the edge of a gentle, winding river, lived a young boy named Oliver. Oliver had always loved the river—it was his favorite place to sit and listen to the soft splashes and whispers of the water as it flowed by, especially at night when everything was quiet and calm. The river sparkled in the moonlight, casting a silvery glow that filled the air with a kind of magic.

Every night, after saying goodnight to his family, Oliver would sit by his window and watch the river, letting its soft murmurs lull him into sleep. He liked to imagine all the secrets the river must hold and all the creatures it must meet along its journey. Tonight, however, the river seemed different. As he sat by his window, he noticed a soft glow on the water's surface.

It flickered gently, like a lantern drifting along the current.

Curiosity got the better of him, and he slipped out of bed, tiptoeing outside to the river's edge. There, in the moonlit water, was a small boat waiting just for him. It was unlike any boat he had ever seen before. The boat had a rounded, cozy shape made from polished wood that gleamed softly under the moonlight. At the front of the boat hung a lantern glowing with a warm, welcoming light.

"Come aboard, Oliver," the river murmured, its voice gentle and comforting, like a lullaby.

Oliver's eyes widened with wonder. He looked around, half-expecting to see someone playing a trick on him, but the river just continued to ripple gently as if it had all the time in the world. With a deep breath, Oliver climbed into the boat, settling onto a soft cushion that felt as warm and cozy as his bed.

As soon as he was settled, the boat began to drift downstream, cradled by the river's soft current. Oliver watched the trees and bushes slip by, their leaves rustling softly as if whispering a quiet goodnight. The lantern cast a gentle glow on the water, creating little sparkles that danced like stars along the river's surface.

As they floated along, Oliver felt the river's gentle rhythm easing his mind as if it were wrapping him in a warm blanket. The river began to hum softly, a melody that seemed to come from everywhere at once, filling the air with a calming, peaceful sound.

"Where are we going?" Oliver asked, his voice barely more than a whisper.

"We're on a journey through the night," the river replied in its gentle voice. "Tonight, I'll show you the world as only the river knows it. You'll meet some of my friends, and they'll share their stories with you."

As the boat drifted around a bend, Oliver saw a family of frogs nestled on a lily pad near the shore. They had round, sleepy faces, and each of them wore a tiny hat made of leaves. One of the frogs looked up, noticing Oliver, and gave a small croak that sounded like a yawn.

"Good evening, young Oliver," the frog said, his voice slow and drowsy. "We're the Froggingtons, and we sing lullabies for the river every night."

The smallest frog, who looked as if he could barely keep his eyes open, began to hum a soft tune, and soon, the whole family joined in. Their voices blended together in a sleepy, soothing melody that made Oliver feel even more relaxed. The tune was gentle and slow, a lullaby that seemed to float on the water, wrapping around him like a cozy blanket.

"Thank you, Froggingtons," Oliver said, his voice soft and full of warmth.

The Froggingtons gave him a sleepy wave as the boat drifted past them, their lullaby lingering in the air, mixing with the river's gentle hum. As they moved further downstream, Oliver felt the rhythm of the boat, the sound of the water, and the lingering lullaby all melting together, lulling him into a state of dreamy calm.

Just ahead, Oliver noticed a large, old turtle resting on a smooth rock by the shore. The turtle had wise, gentle eyes, and his shell was covered with tiny carvings as if it held the stories of a hundred years.

"Hello, Oliver," the turtle greeted him in a slow, deep voice that rumbled like distant thunder. "My name is Tiberius. I've lived by this river for many, many years, and I've seen many things. Would you like to hear a story of the river's journey?"

"Yes, please," Oliver replied, his heart full of wonder.

Tiberius cleared his throat, his voice becoming even softer as he began his tale. "Long ago, before even I was born, the river began its journey from a tiny spring high up in the mountains. It tumbled over rocks and stones, winding through forests and meadows, whispering to the trees and flowers. As it grew, it met all kinds of creatures—deer, rabbits, birds, and even a family of otters who liked to ride its currents."

Oliver listened, mesmerized by the turtle's tale. He could picture the river as a young, playful stream, growing and learning as it flowed through the world. Tiberius continued, "And then, one day, the river met the sea. The waves welcomed it, saying, 'Come, join us, and we will share all our secrets.' But the river loved its journey through the land and wanted to keep flowing, so it said goodbye to the sea and turned back to find its way home."

Oliver's eyelids grew heavy as he listened, his heart warmed by the gentle story. "Thank you, Tiberius," he whispered, feeling as if he, too, were a part of the river's story.

The boat drifted onward, and the sound of Tiberius's voice faded into the night. Oliver felt a deep sense of peace settles over him, a calmness that seemed to come from the river itself.

Soon, the boat passed a grove of trees, their branches arching over the water like a protective canopy. Suddenly, tiny lights appeared among the leaves, flickering on and off like stars scattered through the forest. Oliver realized they were fireflies, their tiny bodies glowing with a soft, golden light.

The fireflies began to dance, their light casting a

gentle glow on the trees and the water below. They floated around the boat, creating a pathway of stars that guided him through the night.

"Good evening, Oliver," a tiny voice called out from somewhere among the lights. "We are the fireflies, and we light the river's path, showing it the way under the night sky."

The fireflies twinkled and flickered, their lights shimmering like tiny stars. Oliver watched in awe as they danced around him, their glow reflecting on the water like a thousand tiny lanterns. The light was soft and soothing, and it filled him with a sense of warmth and comfort.

"Thank you, fireflies," Oliver whispered, his voice barely more than a murmur. The fireflies blinked in response, their lights dimming and brightening as if to say, *You're welcome.*

The boat drifted onward, guided by the gentle light of the fireflies. Oliver felt as though he were floating in a dream, his mind filled with the songs of the Froggingtons, the wise words of Tiberius, and the comforting glow of the fireflies.

As they floated further downstream, the river's current grew even softer, slowing to a gentle, soothing rhythm. The boat glided along, cradling Oliver like a rocking cradle, and he felt himself growing sleepier with every passing moment.

The river murmured a soft lullaby, its voice blending with the sounds of the night. "Close your eyes, dear Oliver," the river whispered, its tone warm and comforting. "Let the night wrap around you like a blanket, and know that you are safe."

Oliver's eyelids grew heavy, his head nodding as he listened to the river's gentle song. He could feel the peace of the night settling over him, wrapping him in a cocoon of warmth and tranquility. The river's soft rhythm lulled him into a dreamy state, and he knew that he would carry this peaceful feeling with him long after he returned home.

As they neared the shore, the boat came to a gentle stop. The river's current slowed to a mere whisper, and the fireflies dimmed their lights, casting a soft glow over the water.

"Thank you for the journey, dear river," Oliver whispered, his voice filled with gratitude and warmth.

The river's voice was soft and kind. "Goodnight, Oliver. May your dreams be as calm and peaceful as the water that flows through the night."

As he stepped out of the boat, a warm, soft blanket appeared around his shoulders, woven from the river's gentle current and the light of the fireflies. Oliver pulled the blanket close, feeling its warmth, and made his way back to his bed, his heart filled with the magic of the night.

When he climbed under his covers, he could still hear the faint whisper of the river, like a lullaby carrying him off to sleep. He closed his eyes, knowing that he would dream of the Froggingtons, Tiberius, the wise old turtle, and the dancing fireflies who lit the way.

And as he drifted into the deepest, most peaceful sleep he'd ever known, Oliver knew that the river would always be there, flowing gently through the night, waiting to share its magic with him again.

# The Cloud King's Lullaby

Tessa was a little girl with a big imagination and a special love for clouds. Every day, she would lie in the grass, staring up at the sky, watching the clouds drift by. She'd point out the ones shaped like animals, castles, or even ships, making up stories about each one. To her, the clouds were magical, as if they were friends that floated up there just to keep her company. Some were fluffy and round, like giant marshmallows, while others were long and wispy, like brushstrokes across the sky. She could watch them for hours, feeling as though they carried secrets of far-off places she'd yet to explore.

One warm evening, as the sun was setting and the sky turned a soft shade of pink and orange, Tessa lay in her bed, pulling her blanket up to her chin. She yawned, feeling her eyes grow heavy, and gazed out her window, where the last traces of sunlight dipped below the horizon. Just as she was about to drift off, a soft, humming sound filled the air. It was a gentle, melodic hum, almost like a lullaby, and it seemed to come from outside her window.

Curious, Tessa climbed out of bed and tiptoed to the window, rubbing her sleepy eyes. As she looked out, she gasped in surprise. Hovering right there, just outside her window, was a fluffy white cloud, softly glowing in the moonlight. It looked like the coziest, fluffiest pillow she'd ever seen, and it was drifting close to her window as if inviting her on a secret adventure.

With a mix of excitement and wonder, Tessa opened the window, letting the cool night breeze swirl around her. She took a deep breath, then carefully climbed onto the cloud, feeling it sink ever so slightly under her weight. It was as soft as she had imagined, cradling her like a gentle hug. The cloud hummed in greeting, a warm, friendly sound that made Tessa feel safe and cozy.

"Hello, Tessa," the cloud seemed to say, though its voice was more of a feeling than a sound. "Are you ready for a journey?"

Tessa nodded, her heart fluttering with excitement. She held on to a small tuft of cloud as it began to float up, drifting higher and higher into the sky. The lights of her house grew smaller below, and the stars above seemed to twinkle in greeting. The cloud carried her gently, like a feather on a breeze, up toward the clouds that she had watched so many times from below.

As they floated higher, Tessa noticed a magnificent sight—there, just above the tallest clouds, was a vast kingdom made entirely of fluffy, glowing clouds. It looked like a magical land of marshmallow castles, cotton candy towers, and bridges made of silver mist. In the center of it all was a grand cloud castle, with turrets that reached toward the stars, surrounded by clouds shaped like animals—lions, bunnies, even dragons—all floating peacefully around it.

At the entrance to the cloud castle stood a giant, friendly-looking cloud with a beard made of rain mist that sparkled in the moonlight. He wore a crown made of stars, which glowed softly atop his head. His face was kind, with eyes that twinkled like distant galaxies.

"Welcome, Tessa," the giant cloud said in a deep, soothing voice. "I am the Cloud King, and this is my kingdom, the Land of Lullabies."

Tessa's eyes widened with wonder as she looked around. "It's beautiful," she whispered, feeling as if she were in a dream.

The Cloud King chuckled, his laughter like the

soft rumble of distant thunder. "Thank you, dear Tessa. This kingdom is where all the world's softest dreams are born. Tonight, we're here to share them with you."

With a gentle wave of his hand, the Cloud King led Tessa further into the Land of Lullabies. They floated along paths made of the fluffiest clouds, where gentle winds hummed melodies that sounded like lullabies drifting through the air. Everywhere she looked, Tessa saw cloud creatures floating by, each with a soft glow and a friendly smile.

The Cloud King stopped beside a cloud shaped like a large, fluffy lion with a mane made of mist. The lion looked sleepy, his eyes half-closed as he floated lazily on a bed of clouds.

"This is Lucky," the Cloud King explained. "He guards the dreams of those who need courage. Every time a child wishes for bravery, Lucky drifts by their window, bringing dreams of strength and courage."

Lucky the cloud lion let out a soft, rumbling purr that sounded like a lullaby. Tessa reached out to pat his fluffy mane, feeling its softness under her fingertips. Lucky blinked slowly, his eyes warm and kind, as if he were thanking her for the gentle touch.

As they continued, they passed a cloud shaped like a bunny, with ears that twitched softly in the breeze.

The bunny had a gentle glow, like moonlight, and it hopped along the clouds, leaving tiny sparkles in its wake.

"This is Luna," the Cloud King said with a smile. "She brings peaceful dreams to those who need rest. When children have had a busy day, Luna visits them, filling their dreams with calm and quiet."

Tessa watched as Luna the bunny floated by, her glow like a soft blanket wrapping around Tessa's heart. She felt a warm, drowsy feeling settle over her, and she let out a contented sigh.

As they walked, Tessa noticed a large, fluffy dragon drifting lazily in the air, its body stretched out like a long, winding river. Its scales were made of wisps of mist, and its eyes sparkled with a gentle light.

"That's Nimbus," the Cloud King said with a nod. "Nimbus brings dreams of adventure to those with big imaginations. When children dream of flying through mountains or exploring new worlds, Nimbus is there, guiding them on their journey."

The dragon gave a slow, graceful nod, his eyes twinkling with kindness. Tessa felt a thrill of excitement just looking at him, and she imagined herself riding on his back, soaring through the clouds, visiting far-off lands.

As they continued their tour, the Cloud King led

Tessa to the highest tower in the cloud castle. Here, the clouds were shaped into musical instruments—a harp made of silvery mist, drums made of fluffy clouds, and a flute that shimmered with a soft, pearly glow. The Cloud King picked up the harp, and with a gentle touch, he began to play a lullaby.

The sound was unlike anything Tessa had ever heard. It was soft and soothing, filling the air with a warmth that made her heart feel light. The other clouds joined in, humming along, creating a melody that seemed to wrap around her like a cozy blanket.

"This is the lullaby we sing to the world every night," the Cloud King explained, his voice deep and soothing. "Each cloud in my kingdom holds a special lullaby, one that travels with the wind and drifts down to every child, filling their dreams with peace."

Tessa closed her eyes, letting the melody wash over her. She felt a sense of calm settle within her, as if all her worries had floated away on the clouds. The lullaby was like a gentle breeze, soft and comforting, carrying her to a place of quiet and rest.

As the song ended, the Cloud King looked down at her with a smile. "Tessa," he said softly, "I have a gift for you. I'll send a piece of this kingdom to visit you each night, so you'll always feel the warmth of the

Land of Lullabies, even when you're back in your room."

He held out his hand, and a small, fluffy cloud appeared, glowing with a soft, silvery light. Tessa reached out and took it, feeling its warmth in her hands.

"Whenever you're ready to sleep, hold this cloud close, and you'll feel the lullabies of my kingdom," the Cloud King promised.

With a final, gentle hug, the Cloud King lifted Tessa onto her fluffy cloud. "It's time to take you back home, little one," he whispered. The cloud began to drift down, cradling her like a pillow as it carried her through the soft, glowing skies.

Tessa felt her eyelids growing heavy, the warmth of the cloud wrapping around her like a blanket. She closed her eyes, feeling the gentle hum of the lullabies in her heart. As the cloud floated back down to her window, she felt herself slipping into the coziest, most peaceful sleep she'd ever known.

When the cloud settled by her window, Tessa climbed back into bed, clutching her little cloud close to her chest. It glowed softly, filling her room with a gentle light, like the warmth of a thousand lullabies.

As she drifted off to sleep, Tessa knew that the Land of Lullabies would always be with her, wrapping her in warmth and peace, filling her dreams with clouds, castles, and the soft, soothing melodies of the Cloud King's lullaby.

And that night, and every night after, she slept with a smile on her face, dreaming of the Land of Lullabies, knowing she'd always have a piece of its magic right by her side.

# The Lighthouse of Dreams

On a tiny island, just beyond the reach of the mainland, stood a tall, old lighthouse. It was known as the Lighthouse of Dreams, and every evening, as the sun dipped below the horizon, it would come alive with a warm, magical light. The golden glow would spread across the sea, stretching like a blanket over the waves, casting a peaceful, comforting light that seemed to soothe everything it touched.

For as long as he could remember, young Leo had been fascinated by the lighthouse. Every night, he would sit by his bedroom window, watching its steady glow shine in the distance. His parents told him that it was just an old lighthouse, there to guide ships safely to shore, but Leo always believed there was something special about it. It was more than a beacon for sailors —it was a keeper of secrets, a guardian of dreams.

One evening, Leo's curiosity got the better of him. The sun had just set, and the lighthouse was beginning to glow, casting its soft, golden light across the water. Leo felt a sudden urge to see it up close, to find out if his childhood suspicions were true. So, with a sense of excitement bubbling inside him, he slipped into a small rowboat by the shore and began rowing toward the island.

The journey across the water was calm and quiet, with only the sound of gentle waves lapping against the boat. As he rowed closer, the lighthouse grew taller and more magnificent, its light casting a warm glow over everything around it. When he finally reached the shore, he tied up his boat and took a deep breath, gazing up at the towering structure before him.

Just as he stepped onto the island, a figure appeared at the base of the lighthouse—a tall, thin man with silvery hair wearing a long, weathered coat. The man's face broke into a kind, welcoming smile, and his eyes sparkled like the night sky.

"Welcome, young Leo," the man said, his voice as soft as the evening breeze. "I've been expecting you."

Leo's eyes widened in surprise. "You know my name?"

The man chuckled, nodding. "Of course. I'm the keeper of this lighthouse, and I know the name of every child who gazes at it with wonder in their heart. My name is Mr. Holden, and I'm delighted to finally meet you."

Leo felt a warmth spread through him, as if the lighthouse's glow had reached right into his chest. "Is it true?" he asked, his voice barely a whisper. "Is there magic in the lighthouse?"

Mr. Holden's eyes twinkled as he nodded. "Oh, yes. The Lighthouse of Dreams is very special. It doesn't just guide ships—it keeps the dreams of everyone on the island safe, shining its light to guard and protect them each night. Would you like to see for yourself?"

Leo nodded eagerly, his heart racing with excitement. Mr. Holden opened the heavy wooden door and gestured for Leo to follow him inside.

As they entered, Leo was immediately filled with awe. The inside of the lighthouse was unlike anything he'd ever seen. The walls were lined with shelves filled with strange and wonderful objects, each one glowing softly under the lighthouse's golden light.

Mr. Holden led Leo up a spiral staircase that wound around the inside of the lighthouse, each step taking him higher and higher, closer to the top. The walls were decorated with carvings of stars, moons, and constellations, and Leo felt as though he were climbing right into the night sky.

At the first landing, Mr. Holden stopped and opened a door to a small room filled with jars. Each jar was filled with a glittering light that sparkled and twinkled like the stars. Leo gasped, his eyes wide with wonder.

"These," Mr. Holden explained, "are jars of dreams. Every night, when the lighthouse glows, it gathers dreams from the hearts of those who are asleep on the island. Each dream is captured and stored here, where it's kept safe until it's ready to return to its dreamer."

Leo walked closer, his fingers hovering over one of the jars. Inside, he could see a tiny, magical scene—a pirate ship sailing across a moonlit sea, its sails billowing as it chased after a distant treasure. He watched in amazement as the tiny ship moved within the jar, as if it were alive.

"This one belongs to a boy who dreams of being a pirate," Mr. Holden said with a smile. "Every time he closes his eyes, he sets sail on adventures across the seven seas."

Leo moved to another jar, where he saw a little girl dancing with fairies under a silver moon. The fairies' wings glowed like fireflies, and the girl twirled happily, her face lit with joy.

"And this one belongs to a girl who dreams of dancing with fairies," Mr. Holden explained. "Each dream is special, and each one has its own magic."

Leo felt his heart swell with wonder as he looked around the room, taking in the countless jars of dreams, each one a tiny world of its own. He could have stayed there forever, watching the dreams dance and sparkle, but Mr. Holden gently placed a hand on his shoulder.

"Come, there's more to see," he said, leading Leo back to the staircase.

They continued their climb, and as they reached the next landing, Mr. Holden opened another door. Inside, they found shelves lined with shells—smooth, polished shells in every color imaginable. Each shell had a soft glow, as if it held a tiny piece of moonlight.

"These are enchanted shells," Mr. Holden said, his voice low and reverent. "Each one has listened to the secrets of the sea, capturing the dreams of the ocean itself. When sailors pass by, the shells share these dreams with them, guiding them safely to shore."

Leo picked up a small, pearly shell and held it to his ear. As he listened, he heard the soft, soothing sound of waves crashing against the shore, mixed with the faintest whisper of a lullaby. It was a sound that filled him with a sense of calm, as if he were lying on a beach under the stars, listening to the ocean's gentle song.

He put the shell back on the shelf, his heart filled with gratitude for the magic it held. Mr. Holden gave him a warm smile, then guided him further up the stairs.

At the very top of the lighthouse, they reached the final room, where the great light of the lighthouse shone brightly. The room was filled with an other-worldly glow, casting soft shadows that danced along the walls. In the center of the room was a large, gleaming crystal that pulsed with a warm, golden light.

"This," Mr. Holden said, placing a hand on the crystal, "is the heart of the Lighthouse of Dreams. It's what makes everything possible. The light from this crystal reaches across the island, wrapping every home and every child in a blanket of peace and comfort. It guides their dreams, helping them find their way to the places they long to visit."

Leo gazed at the crystal in awe, feeling its warmth radiate through him. He could almost feel the dreams flowing through it, like rivers of light, each one filled with joy, wonder, and peace.

Mr. Holden placed a gentle hand on Leo's shoulder, his face soft and kind. "Would you like a piece of dreamlight to take home with you?" he asked, his voice barely more than a whisper.

Leo nodded, his heart full of gratitude. Mr. Holden reached into his pocket and pulled out a small, glowing stone, no larger than a pebble. It shimmered with a soft, golden light, and when Leo held it in his hand, he felt a warmth spread through him, filling him with a sense of calm and wonder.

"This stone holds a piece of the lighthouse's magic," Mr. Holden explained. "Keep it beside your bed, and it will watch over you as you sleep, guiding your dreams just as the lighthouse guides the dreams of the island."

Leo clutched the stone close, his heart swelling with joy. "Thank you, Mr. Holden," he said, his voice full of warmth. "I'll keep it safe."

With a gentle smile, Mr. Holden led Leo back down the staircase, each step filled with a sense of peace and contentment. When they reached the door, Mr. Holden gave him a final, kind pat on the shoulder.

"Goodnight, Leo," he said softly. "Remember, the lighthouse will always be here, watching over your dreams."

Leo stepped out of the lighthouse and back onto the beach, the stone glowing softly in his hand. As he climbed into his rowboat and began to row back home, he felt a deep sense of calm wash over him. The lighthouse's light shone brightly behind him, casting a golden glow over the water, guiding him safely back to shore.

When he reached the mainland, Leo climbed into bed, placing the glowing stone on his bedside table. Its light filled his room with a soft, gentle glow, and he felt as if the lighthouse were right there beside him, watching over him as he drifted into sleep.

That night, and every night after, Leo slept soundly, his dreams filled with magical worlds and gentle lullabies, knowing that the Lighthouse of Dreams would always be there to keep him safe. And as he closed his eyes, he whispered a quiet thank you, feeling the lighthouse's light wrap around him like a warm blanket, guiding him into the sweetest of dreams.

# The Moon's Sleepy Garden

In a small village nestled between the hills and a quiet forest, lived a little girl named Mira. Mira was seven years old and full of curiosity, with a brave heart and a deep love for nature. She spent her days exploring the woods near her home, finding hidden paths, and watching birds and animals go about their days. Every night, she would gaze out her window at the moon, wondering what secrets it might hold, and imagining the world it watched over from so high above.

One evening, Mira noticed something strange. It was a full moon, round and bright, casting a silver light that seemed to dance across the trees. As she looked closer, she saw a soft, shimmering path of moonlight stretching from her window, weaving its way into the forest like a ribbon of stardust. The path glowed with a gentle, silvery light, beckoning her with a quiet invitation.

Her heart fluttered with excitement and curiosity. Without a second thought, Mira slipped out of bed, tiptoed through the house, and stepped outside into the cool night air. She followed the moonlit path into the woods, each step filling her with wonder and a sense of adventure. The forest was calm, with only the soft sounds of night creatures rustling in the leaves and the gentle hoot of an owl in the distance.

As she walked along the path, Mira noticed that the trees and bushes seemed to glow with a faint light, as if they were bathed in moonlight. The leaves shimmered like silver, and the air was filled with a soft, musical hum. It was as though the whole forest were singing a lullaby.

Finally, the moonlit path led her to a hidden grove, surrounded by tall trees and bathed in the softest glow she had ever seen. Mira gasped in awe. This was no ordinary grove—she had stumbled upon the Moon's Sleepy Garden.

The garden was a magical place that seemed to come alive only in the light of the full moon. Flowers of every shape and size bloomed in silvery hues, their petals shimmering as if dusted with stardust. There were plants with long, delicate leaves that swayed gently, as if dancing to a silent melody, and bushes covered in tiny, glowing berries that looked like miniature stars.

As she took in the beauty around her, a soft voice whispered in her ear, as light as a breeze. "Welcome, Mira."

Mira looked around, her eyes wide with wonder, and saw a tiny moonbeam floating beside her, glowing like a sliver of silver light. It had a friendly, gentle face and eyes that sparkled like stars.

"Hello," Mira whispered, not wanting to break the peacefulness of the garden. "Who are you?"

"I am Moony," the moonbeam replied with a warm smile. "This is the Moon's Sleepy Garden, a special place that only appears when the moon is full. Tonight, the garden needs a little help to fall asleep. Would you like to help me?"

Mira's heart swelled with excitement. "Yes, I'd love to help!"

Moony floated ahead, guiding her deeper into the garden. The air was filled with the scent of night-blooming flowers, and a gentle breeze made the leaves rustle softly, like the whisper of a lullaby.

They came to a patch of glowing flowers with soft, rounded petals, each one swaying slightly, as if it were too drowsy to stay still. Moony gestured to the flowers with a tiny nod.

"These flowers are having trouble settling down," Moony explained. "They need a gentle touch to help them close their petals for the night."

Mira knelt beside the flowers and reached out her hand, gently brushing her fingers over their soft petals. She whispered a quiet goodnight to each one, and as she did, the flowers began to close, their petals folding in like sleepy eyelids.

"Goodnight, little flowers," Mira murmured, her voice soft and calming.

The flowers sighed softly, their glow dimming as they drifted into slumber. Moony floated beside her, a look of contentment in its twinkling eyes. "Well done, Mira. The flowers are ready to sleep."

They moved on, and soon, they came to a tree with long, sweeping branches that swayed gently in the breeze. Nestled among the branches were tiny birds with feathers that glowed like moonlight. They were tucked into their nests, but they shifted restlessly, unable to fully settle.

"These birds need a lullaby," Moony whispered. "Would you sing them a song to help them fall asleep?"

Mira smiled, feeling warmth spread through her heart. She began to hum a soft, gentle tune, the kind of melody her mother would hum to her when she was very little. The sound floated through the air like a breeze, wrapping around the little birds in their nests.

One by one, the birds nestled deeper into their feathers, their tiny eyes closing as they drifted off to sleep. Mira watched as they stilled, their breathing soft and steady, like the rhythm of the garden itself.

"Thank you, Mira," Moony whispered, its voice full of warmth. "The birds are at peace."

As they continued through the garden, Mira noticed a group of leaves rustling softly, as if they were chattering to one another. The leaves trembled in the moonlight, their silvery edges shimmering with each tiny movement.

"These leaves need a gentle touch to help them quiet down," Moony explained, floating closer. "Would you brush them softly, just like you did with the flowers?"

Mira reached out, running her fingers over the leaves, brushing them as softly as a feather. As her fingers touched them, the leaves stopped trembling, their edges growing still and calm. They seemed to sigh in relief, settling into a gentle, peaceful state.

With each rustling leaf and each drowsy flower, Mira felt a calmness settle over her. She realized that helping the garden fall asleep was making her feel sleepy, too, as if the magic of the place was wrapping her in a blanket of peace.

Moony continued guiding her through the garden, and soon, they reached a small pool of water, its surface as smooth as glass. The pool reflected the moon, casting a soft, silver light over everything around it. At the edge of the pool were tiny flowers with petals that glowed like stars.

"These flowers need a sprinkle of stardust," Moony said with a gentle smile. "Would you like to gather some?"

Mira nodded eagerly, her eyes shining with excitement. She reached into a small pouch that Moony handed her, gathering a handful of sparkling stardust. It felt cool and soft in her hand, like powdered moonlight.

She sprinkled the stardust over the flowers, watching as it settled on their petals. The flowers glowed brighter for a moment, then slowly began to close, their petals folding in as they drifted into a peaceful sleep.

"Goodnight, little stars," Mira whispered, her heart full of warmth.

The garden grew quieter, each plant and creature settling into slumber. Mira felt her own eyelids growing heavy, the peacefulness of the garden wrapping around her like a soft, cozy blanket.

Moony floated beside her, its gentle light casting a warm glow over her face. "You've done a wonderful job, Mira," it said softly. "The garden is at peace, and now it's time for you to rest, too."

Mira yawned, feeling the calmness of the garden settling deep within her. She looked around, taking in the beauty of the Moon's Sleepy Garden one last time, feeling grateful to have been a part of its magic.

"Thank you, Moony," she whispered. "I'll never forget this night."

Moony smiled, wrapping its light around her like a warm embrace. "And we'll never forget you, Mira. Whenever you look at the moon, remember the garden and know that it's always there, waiting for you."

With a gentle glow, Moony began to lead her back along the moonlit path. As they walked, the trees and flowers glowed softly, their light fading as they drifted further into sleep. Mira felt the calmness of the night settle over her, filling her with a sense of peace and wonder.

When they reached the edge of the forest, Moony gave her a final, warm hug. "Goodnight, Mira," it whispered. "Sweet dreams."

Mira smiled, feeling as though she were wrapped in

a blanket of moonlight. She waved goodbye to Moony, then made her way back to her house, her heart full of warmth and wonder.

As she climbed into bed, Mira pulled her blanket up to her chin, feeling the peacefulness of the garden still with her. She closed her eyes, imagining the Moon's Sleepy Garden, with its glowing flowers, gentle birds, and rustling leaves.

And as she drifted into sleep, she dreamed of the magical garden under the light of the full moon, knowing that it would always be there, waiting for her on nights when the moon was full and the stars were bright.

# The Sleepy Train's Starry Route

Floyd was a boy with a boundless imagination and a deep love for trains. Every day, he would spend hours playing with his toy train set, dreaming of traveling to faraway places where the tracks stretched endlessly under the stars. He'd even look out his bedroom window at night, watching for any sign of a train in the distance, hoping that maybe, just maybe, one would appear for him.

One evening, after an especially busy day of play, Floyd climbed into bed, pulling his blanket up to his chin. He was just starting to drift off when he heard something faint outside his window—a soft, rhythmic chugging sound. His eyes snapped open, and he sat up, his heart racing with excitement. The sound grew louder, the gentle "chugga-chugga" of an engine coming closer, like a lullaby in motion.

Curious, Floyd slipped out of bed and tiptoed over to his window. There, glimmering in the soft glow of moonlight, was a cozy little train waiting just outside, nestled in a bed of starlight. It was unlike any train he'd ever seen before. The locomotive had a warm, welcoming glow, and the carriages looked like the comfiest seats, covered in soft, plush cushions that practically invited you to sink into them.

With a mixture of awe and excitement, Floyd opened his window. He barely had to stretch as a friendly voice called out from one of the carriages, "Well, hop on, Floyd! We've got a starry route to explore tonight!"

Floyd's heart leaped with joy. He climbed out the window and into the carriage, feeling the cozy cushions envelop him as he settled into his seat. Just then, an owl wearing a tiny conductor's cap appeared, offering him a warm, soft blanket and a small, steaming cup of something that smelled like cocoa with a hint of magic.

"Welcome aboard the Sleepy Train!" the owl conductor said with a kind, twinkling smile. "I'm Ollie, your conductor for the night. Here's some star-dust cocoa to keep you warm, and a blanket made from the softest clouds. We're off on a journey through the stars, so snuggle in and enjoy the ride."

Floyd took a sip of the stardust cocoa, feeling warmth spread through him from his head to his toes. It tasted like chocolate and a sprinkle of magic, making him feel cozy and calm all at once. He wrapped the cloud-soft blanket around his shoulders and leaned back, gazing out the window as the train began to move.

With a gentle "chugga-chugga," the Sleepy Train rolled forward, gliding smoothly along a path that seemed to float in the sky itself. Stars twinkled all around them, some so close that Floyd felt he could reach out and touch them. The train entered a sky-blue tunnel, and constellations lined the walls like lanterns guiding them along.

Floyd looked out and saw his first passenger, a family of squirrels nestled together on one of the plush seats. Each squirrel had a tiny acorn pillow, and they snuggled close, their little eyes drooping as they yawned. One of the baby squirrels gave a tiny wave to Floyd, before curling up and drifting into a gentle sleep.

Ollie the owl noticed Floyd watching them and chuckled softly. "They're regulars on the Sleepy

Train," he said with a wink. "Nothing like a nighttime journey to lull them to sleep."

The train hummed along, a soft lullaby filling the air. The gentle chugging of the engine and the faint hum of the tracks created a rhythm that made Floyd's eyelids feel just a little heavier. He took another sip of his cocoa and sighed happily, feeling warmth and peace wrap around him like a cocoon.

As they continued, the Sleepy Train passed a cloud that looked like a floating bed, draped in silver mist. Lying on it was a little rabbit, wrapped up in a cozy scarf. He blinked sleepily at Floyd, giving a small, soft nod before closing his eyes and resting his head on a fluffy patch of cloud.

"We have a lot of sleepy travelers tonight," Ollie said, glancing fondly at the rabbit. "That's Pippin, the rabbit. He hops on every now and then when he needs a little extra warmth. The Sleepy Train takes care of all kinds of passengers."

The train gently floated over clouds, gliding as if it were skating on air. They passed under the sparkling arch of the Milky Way, which stretched across the sky like a glowing bridge. The stars twinkled in patterns that seemed to wave as they passed, as if welcoming them into their quiet, starlit world.

Floyd gazed up in wonder, feeling as though he

were traveling through a dream. The train dipped and rose softly, cradling him like a gentle lullaby. With each turn, he felt his heart fill with a warmth that seemed to flow from the stars themselves.

Just then, a faint glow appeared in the sky, growing brighter as they approached. It was a constellation shaped like a bear, its stars shining like little lanterns. The bear seemed to be waving, and Floyd smiled, waving back.

"Ah, that's Ursa Major," Ollie explained. "He watches over this route, making sure all our passengers have safe and peaceful journeys."

The train continued along its gentle path, and soon they passed a group of glowing starfish floating by, each one casting a soft light as it drifted in the sky like a sleepy parade. Floyd watched in wonder as they glowed in shades of soft blue and purple, their lights shimmering like tiny stars.

"They're on their way to the Starry Sea," Ollie said in a hushed tone, as if not to disturb them. "It's where the stars rest before they shine for the night."

The sight made Floyd feel calm, as if he, too, were being carried along on a gentle wave. He leaned back, sinking deeper into the plush seat, feeling the peace of the Sleepy Train wrapping around him.

As they continued, the train began to slow, gliding

through a tunnel made of soft clouds. The clouds floated around them, casting a faint, misty glow, as if they were passing through a magical world hidden just beyond the stars. Ollie pulled a small lever, and a soft lullaby began to play, its notes filling the air like a gentle breeze.

The lullaby made Floyd's eyes grow heavy, the warm blanket and soft cushion lulling him into a drowsy state. He felt as though he were drifting along with the train, floating on a wave of dreams.

Just then, Ollie leaned over with a gentle smile. "We're almost at our last stop, Floyd," he whispered softly. "But don't worry—the Sleepy Train will always be here, waiting to take you on another journey whenever you need it."

Floyd smiled sleepily, feeling a wave of warmth and gratitude fill his heart. He had never felt so calm, so wrapped up in peace. The stars outside glowed like old friends, each one twinkling as if saying goodnight.

As the train came to a gentle stop, Ollie helped Floyd climb out of the carriage. They were back at his window, the soft glow of the train casting a warm light over his room. Ollie handed him a tiny, glowing stone that felt warm in his hand.

"A little gift from the Sleepy Train," Ollie said with

a wink. "Keep this by your bed, and you'll always have a piece of starlight with you."

Floyd thanked Ollie with a hug, feeling a sense of calm wash over him. He climbed back through his window, tucking the glowing stone under his pillow, and snuggled into bed.

As he closed his eyes, he could still hear the faint chugging of the Sleepy Train as it drifted away, carrying its passengers off into the night. Floyd drifted off to sleep with a smile, his dreams filled with cozy carriages, stardust cocoa, and the gentle hum of the Sleepy Train's starry route.

And that night, and many nights after, Floyd dreamed of the Sleepy Train, knowing it would always be there to take him on adventures through the stars, wrapping him in peace and warmth with every journey.

# The Sleepy Sandcastle Kingdom

It was a perfect summer night at the beach, and eight-year-old Ivy lay snuggled up in her sleeping bag, listening to the soft crash of waves on the shore. She was camping with her family just a few feet from the edge of the ocean, under a blanket of stars. The air was warm, and the salty breeze tickled her nose, carrying with it the mysterious, soothing whispers of the sea. As she closed her eyes, she imagined the waves were telling stories to the sand, ancient tales of sunken ships, hidden treasures, and underwater kingdoms.

Just as she was drifting into sleep, Ivy heard a faint, tinkling sound coming from the shore, almost like tiny bells. Curious, she sat up and peered out of her tent, her eyes adjusting to the silvery glow of the moonlight.

The beach was quiet and still, except for a faint shimmer near the water's edge.

With her heart pounding in excitement, Ivy slipped out of her tent, her bare feet sinking into the cool, soft sand. She followed the shimmering trail, feeling as though she were walking in a dream. As she got closer to the water, she noticed something incredible—a sandcastle kingdom, glowing softly in the moonlight, had appeared at the edge of the shore.

The kingdom was unlike anything Ivy had ever seen before. Towers and turrets made of fine, silvery sand rose high into the night sky, adorned with seashells that glowed like tiny lanterns. Delicate bridges connected the towers, arching gracefully over pools of water that sparkled with a thousand tiny lights, like stars reflecting on the ocean's surface.

Ivy's eyes widened in wonder. "It's beautiful," she whispered.

Just then, she noticed a small, golden figure scuttling toward her. It was a hermit crab, his shell shimmering in the moonlight like polished gold. The crab wore a tiny crown made of seaweed and held a little staff made of coral.

"Welcome to the Sleepy Sandcastle Kingdom!" the hermit crab greeted her in a cheerful, gentle voice. "I'm

Sandy, the royal guide of this magical realm. I've been waiting for you, Ivy."

Ivy gasped in surprise. "You know my name?"

Sandy gave her a warm, knowing smile. "Oh, yes. Only those who believe in the magic of the sea can find their way here. The ocean told me you'd be coming tonight."

Ivy's heart swelled with joy. She had always believed there was something magical about the ocean, and now she was here, in a place where dreams came to life. "Will you show me around?" she asked, excitement bubbling in her voice.

"Of course!" Sandy replied, gesturing with his coral staff. "Come along, and I'll take you on a tour of our enchanted kingdom."

With Sandy leading the way, Ivy stepped into the sandcastle city, her feet sinking gently into the soft, warm sand. They passed by a grand gate made of seashells, each one glowing with a soft, pearly light. Ivy noticed that the shells seemed to hum a gentle melody, like a lullaby, filling the air with a peaceful, calming sound.

Sandy led her through winding paths lined with delicate sand sculptures of dolphins, seahorses, and other sea creatures, each one glowing softly in the moonlight. They reached a square where tiny lanterns hung from poles made of driftwood, casting a warm glow over everything.

"Look up, Ivy," Sandy said with a wink. "This is the Airy Lagoon, where our very special sand creatures float."

Ivy tilted her head back, and her eyes sparkled with wonder. Floating gently above them were shimmering jellyfish, their tentacles trailing softly through the air like ribbons. Each jellyfish glowed with a soft, dreamy light, casting a gentle glow over the sand below.

"They look like stars," Ivy murmured, mesmerized.

"They're our very own Sleepy Stars," Sandy explained. "They drift through the air, filling the kingdom with a peaceful glow. They're here to help everyone feel calm and ready for sleep."

The jellyfish moved gracefully, drifting in slow circles above them, their soft glow making Ivy feel as if she were wrapped in a warm blanket of starlight. She could feel her own eyelids growing a little heavier, lulled by the jellyfish's gentle rhythm.

Sandy led her further into the kingdom, and they passed by a sandy garden filled with tiny, twinkling starfish nestled among seaweed beds. The starfish seemed to be singing a soft, melodic lullaby, their tiny voices blending into a harmonious tune that made Ivy's heart feel warm and content.

"They're singing the ocean's lullaby," Sandy whispered. "The starfish sing every night to help the waves lull all the sea creatures into a gentle sleep."

Ivy closed her eyes for a moment, letting the soft lullaby wash over her. She could feel the ocean's rhythm in the song, a gentle ebb and flow that matched the waves lapping against the shore. It was as if the entire ocean were cradling her, filling her with peace and calm.

As they continued, Sandy led her to the tallest tower in the kingdom, a grand castle made entirely of silvery sand that shimmered under the moonlight. Ivy looked up in awe, marveling at its graceful spires and delicate archways.

"This is the Dream Castle," Sandy said softly. "It's where we keep all of the ocean's dreams safe."

They entered the castle, and Ivy's eyes widened in amazement. Inside, the walls were lined with small, glistening jars, each one filled with a different light. Some jars held a soft blue glow, others a warm pink, and still others shimmered with a gentle golden light.

"These are the dreams of the sea creatures," Sandy explained. "Each one is filled with a different kind of dream. Some hold dreams of adventure, others of peace, and some of gentle laughter and play."

Ivy wandered through the room, gazing at each jar

in wonder. She reached out to touch one that glowed with a warm, golden light, feeling its soft warmth spread through her fingers.

"This one belongs to a little dolphin," Sandy said with a smile. "She dreams of leaping through sparkling waves, racing alongside her friends under the sun."

Ivy felt her heart fill with happiness as she imagined the little dolphin playing in the water, her dreams alive and safe in the jar. She looked at another jar, this one a soft blue, and could almost see a gentle turtle drifting through a coral reef, her heart filled with peace.

They left the Dream Castle, and Sandy guided her down to a small, hidden cove where the waves whispered secrets to the sand. Ivy could hear the soft murmur of the tide, its voice calm and steady, like a lullaby sung by the sea itself.

"The ocean sings every night," Sandy explained, his voice barely more than a whisper. "Its song is what helps all the creatures of the sea drift off to sleep. The waves carry dreams from shore to shore, like little boats filled with starlight."

Ivy closed her eyes, listening to the soothing sound of the waves. She felt as though the ocean's song were wrapping around her, filling her with a deep sense of calm and warmth.

As they sat by the cove, Ivy leaned against a smooth rock, letting the cool, salty breeze wash over her. She could feel the magic of the Sleepy Sandcastle Kingdom all around her, a world where dreams floated like bubbles, and every creature was cradled in the gentle rhythm of the ocean.

Sandy turned to her with a kind smile. "The Sleepy Sandcastle Kingdom is always here, Ivy, waiting for those who believe in the magic of the sea. Anytime you want to return, just close your eyes and listen to the waves. They'll guide you back to us."

Ivy smiled, feeling her eyelids growing heavy. "Thank you, Sandy. This is the most wonderful place I've ever been."

With a gentle nod, Sandy handed her a small, shimmering shell. It glowed softly, like a tiny piece of moonlight. "Keep this by your bed," he said, "and you'll always have a little piece of the ocean's dreams with you."

Ivy clutched the shell close, feeling its warmth in her hands. She yawned, her body sinking into a sleepy state, as if the sand itself were cradling her. The soft lullaby of the ocean filled her ears, and the glow of the sandcastle kingdom surrounded her like a warm embrace.

As she closed her eyes, Ivy felt herself drifting into

sleep, her dreams filled with glowing jellyfish, singing starfish, and the soft, soothing whispers of the waves.

And as she slipped into a deep, peaceful slumber, Ivy knew that the Sleepy Sandcastle Kingdom would always be there, waiting for her by the shore, a magical world of dreams cradled by the sea.

# The Slumbering Snow Globe

Ella loved snow globes. Each one was a tiny world captured in glass, swirling with glittery snow whenever she shook it. She had a shelf in her room dedicated just to her collection—there was one with a snowy cabin in the woods, another with a cheerful snowman in a town square, and even one with a sparkling castle surrounded by evergreens. But among all her snow globes, there was one that was especially mysterious.

This snow globe had been a gift from her grandmother, who had given it to her last winter. It was larger than any other globe she had, with a gentle, warm glow that seemed to come from inside. Her grandmother had told her that it was a special snow globe, one that didn't need to be shaken to make the snow fall. "One day, when the time is right, this snow globe will reveal its secrets," her grandmother had said with a smile.

Ella had always wondered what that meant. Every now and then, she would take the globe down from its shelf and gaze into it, hoping to catch a glimpse of whatever secrets it held. But nothing ever happened—until one cold winter night when the snow was falling softly outside her window.

Wrapped in a cozy blanket, Ella sat on her bed, holding the glowing snow globe in her hands. The room was quiet, and the only light came from the soft glow of the snow globe. As she gazed into it, she noticed something different. The snow inside the globe wasn't just sitting still—it was moving, falling slowly like real snowflakes. She blinked in surprise, watching as the tiny flakes drifted down, sparkling as they settled onto the ground inside the globe.

And then, before she knew it, something truly magical happened. The world around her began to shift and shimmer as if she were looking through frosted glass. She felt herself getting smaller, shrinking down until she was tiny, and with a soft whoosh, she slipped inside the snow globe.

When Ella opened her eyes, she found herself standing in the middle of a cozy, snowy village. The air was filled with the gentle scent of pine, and fluffy snowflakes drifted down slowly from the sky, each one sparkling like a tiny star. The snow under her feet was soft, like the fluffiest blanket, and everywhere she looked, there were little houses with warm, golden light shining from their windows.

The village was peaceful, wrapped in the quiet hush of falling snow. It was as if she had stepped into a dream.

As Ella took in the beautiful scene, she heard a soft voice behind her. "Welcome, Ella. We've been expecting you."

Turning around, she saw a wise-looking fox with fur as white as the snow and eyes that twinkled like stars. He wore a scarf made of blue wool and had a gentle smile on his face.

"Who are you?" Ella asked, her voice filled with wonder.

"I am the Snow Keeper," the fox replied, bowing slightly. "I watch over the Slumbering Snow Globe and all the peaceful dreams within it. This village is a place of rest, where every snowflake holds a wish for warmth and comfort."

Ella's heart filled with warmth at his words. "It's so beautiful here," she said, looking around at the cozy lights and gently falling snow.

The Snow Keeper nodded. "Would you like to

help me prepare the village for the night?" he asked kindly. "It's almost time for all the creatures here to settle in for a cozy sleep."

Ella nodded eagerly. She loved the idea of helping the gentle animals of this magical village get ready for bed. The Snow Keeper led her through the snowy streets, which glowed with a soft, golden light from lanterns hanging on posts. The light cast warm shadows on the snow, making everything feel safe and snug.

Their first stop was a little cottage nestled between two snowy pines. A small polar bear cub, wearing a scarf that was almost as big as he was, peeked out from the doorway. He let out a tiny yawn, his eyes drooping sleepily.

"Good evening, little one," the Snow Keeper said with a smile. "Are you ready for bed?"

The polar bear cub nodded, rubbing his eyes with a paw. Ella knelt down, giving the cub a gentle pat on the head. "Let's tuck you in, shall we?" she said softly.

She followed the cub inside his cozy cottage, where a tiny bed made of soft pine branches and fluffy snow awaited him. Ella helped the cub snuggle into bed, pulling a tiny quilt over him. The quilt was decorated with stars and moons, and as she tucked him in, it seemed to glow with a warm, comforting light.

"Sweet dreams, little one," she whispered. The polar bear cub let out another tiny yawn, curling up under his quilt as his eyes slowly closed.

As they left the cottage, the Snow Keeper turned to Ella with a twinkle in his eye. "You're a natural at this," he said warmly. "Would you like to meet the other creatures in the village?"

Ella's face lit up with excitement. "Yes, please!"

They continued through the village, visiting each cozy little home. In one house, they found a family of tiny penguins, each wearing a colorful scarf. The penguins were already tucked into bed, but they chirped happily when they saw Ella, thanking her with soft, sleepy voices. Ella smiled, giving each penguin a gentle pat on the head as they snuggled into their soft, snowy beds.

Next, they stopped by a small, round burrow where a sleepy rabbit was nodding off in her chair, wrapped in a fluffy scarf. Ella gently guided her to her bed, tucking a soft blanket around her shoulders as the rabbit murmured a sleepy "Thank you."

As they continued, the snow kept falling softly around them, settling onto the rooftops and blanketing the village in a peaceful hush. Ella noticed that each snowflake seemed to glow with a tiny light, like a little wish floating down from the sky.

"What makes the snowflakes glow like that?" she asked the Snow Keeper.

The wise fox smiled. "Each snowflake holds a wish for rest, warmth, and peaceful dreams," he explained. "When they fall, they bring a sense of calm to everyone they touch. It's part of what makes the Slumbering Snow Globe such a peaceful place."

Ella looked up, watching the glowing snowflakes drift down. She felt as if each flake was bringing her a little bit of warmth and calm, filling her heart with peace.

Their final stop was a large tree in the center of the village. At its base was a small den, where a gentle old owl was waiting, his feathers dusted with snow. He wore a pair of tiny glasses and looked at Ella with kind, sleepy eyes.

"Good evening, Mr. Owl," the Snow Keeper greeted him. "It's time to settle in for the night."

The owl nodded, his eyes twinkling behind his glasses. "Thank you, Snow Keeper," he murmured in a voice as soft as the snow. "And who is this young helper?"

"This is Ella," the Snow Keeper replied. "She's helping us prepare the village for a peaceful sleep."

The owl gave Ella a nod of approval. "It's a pleasure to meet you, my dear. Thank you for bringing warmth to our little village."

Ella smiled, feeling a warm glow in her heart. She helped the owl settle onto his cozy perch, tucking a small, knitted blanket around his feathers. The owl let out a soft hoot of thanks before closing his eyes, drifting into a gentle slumber.

As they walked back through the village, Ella noticed that all the lights in the cottages were slowly dimming, casting a soft, golden glow over the snow. The whole village was quiet, wrapped in the peaceful hush of night.

The Snow Keeper stopped in the center of the village, looking down at Ella with a kind smile. "Thank you for your help, Ella. You've brought a great deal of warmth and comfort to our sleepy little town."

Ella felt a wave of drowsiness wash over her, the soft glow of the village filling her with a sense of calm. "Thank you for letting me help," she whispered, stifling a yawn.

The Snow Keeper chuckled softly. "It's time for you to rest now, too," he said gently. "But don't worry —this village will always be here, waiting for you whenever you need a place of peace and warmth."

As he spoke, Ella felt herself becoming lighter, as though she were floating on a soft cloud. The village around her began to blur, its lights twinkling softly like stars. She closed her eyes, feeling the warmth of the snowflakes settling around her like a cozy blanket.

When she opened her eyes, she was back in her room, still holding the warm, glowing snow globe in her hands. She looked down at it, feeling a sense of calm and peace in her heart, as if a piece of the village had stayed with her.

Ella placed the snow globe on her bedside table, the soft glow casting a gentle light over her room. She climbed into bed, pulling her blanket up to her chin, and closed her eyes, feeling as though she were back in the snowy village, with the soft snowflakes drifting down around her.

As she drifted into sleep, her dreams were filled with the cozy cottages, friendly animals, and the peaceful glow of the Slumbering Snow Globe. And every time she looked at the snow globe after that night, she felt a warm, quiet calm, knowing that the village of peaceful dreams was always there, waiting for her to visit again.

# The River of Rainbow Dreams

Jonah loved colors. He loved the reds and yellows of autumn leaves, the bright blues of the sky, and the greens of the forest. But most of all, he loved to paint. Every afternoon, he would take his paints and brushes outside, finding inspiration in the colors around him. He painted the trees, the flowers, and even the little animals that scurried about, bringing each of them to life on his canvas with swirls of color.

One afternoon, while exploring a path he'd never taken before, Jonah stumbled upon something extraordinary. At the edge of the forest, he found a shimmering river, unlike any he had ever seen. Its surface sparkled and gleamed with an array of colors, shifting and changing like a rainbow caught in a gentle breeze. The colors flowed together in a magical dance, swirling in hues of red, orange, yellow, green, blue, and purple.

Jonah's eyes sparkled with wonder. He reached out to touch the water, but as his fingers neared the surface, a gentle warmth seemed to radiate from the river, as if inviting him closer. He spent hours by the river, watching the colors shift and blend, and when the sun began to set, he finally returned home, his mind still buzzing with the memory of the magical river.

That night, as he climbed into bed, he couldn't stop thinking about the colors. He closed his eyes, imagining the river flowing through his dreams, a place where colors came to life in ways he had never seen before.

Just as he was drifting off to sleep, he heard a soft, soothing sound, like the gentle flow of water. He opened his eyes and gasped—the shimmering, rainbow-colored river was right there, beside his bed, glowing softly in the moonlight. A gentle breeze carried the scent of wildflowers, filling his room with a calm, comforting warmth.

"Come, Jonah," a soft voice whispered, as gentle as the flow of the river. "Join us on a journey through the colors of dreams."

Before he knew it, Jonah had slipped out of bed

and was stepping toward the river. A large, soft lily pad floated beside him, glowing with a pale, silvery light. It was wide and sturdy, and as he climbed onto it, it gently dipped and then lifted him, floating on the surface of the river.

The lily pad began to drift downstream, carrying Jonah along the colorful, glowing waters. The river seemed alive with magic, each bend and curve glowing with a new, brilliant color. He settled onto the lily pad, feeling as if he were wrapped in a cozy blanket made of dreams.

As he drifted along, the first part of the river glowed with a serene, deep blue. The color surrounded him, filling the air with a calm, peaceful feeling. In the blue waters, Jonah noticed playful shapes gliding beneath the surface—dolphins, their graceful bodies gliding in and out of the water with quiet elegance.

One of the dolphins leapt up beside his lily pad, splashing softly and sending tiny droplets that sparkled like stars. The dolphin had kind, sleepy eyes and a gentle smile.

"Hello, Jonah," the dolphin said in a voice as soft as a lullaby. "Welcome to the blue part of the River of Rainbow Dreams. Here, we bring dreams of the sea, of waves and calm waters."

The dolphin gave a slow, graceful twirl, and as it

dove back into the water, Jonah felt a wave of peace wash over him. He imagined himself drifting on the ocean, feeling the gentle rise and fall of the waves, surrounded by the endless, soothing blue.

"Thank you," Jonah whispered, his voice filled with calm. The dolphins swam beside him for a while, guiding him gently along the blue river until he saw the water begin to change to a soft, grassy green.

As he entered the green part of the river, he heard a gentle croaking sound. Looking around, he saw a family of frogs perched on rocks and lily pads along the river's edge, each one wearing a tiny crown made of leaves. The frogs greeted him with slow, sleepy croaks, their voices harmonizing into a soft, soothing lullaby.

One of the frogs, a wise-looking creature with big, gentle eyes, hopped onto his lily pad. "Welcome to the green part of the river, Jonah," the frog said with a deep, warm croak. "Here, we bring dreams of forests, where trees sway and leaves rustle in a gentle breeze."

The frog closed its eyes and began to hum a soft tune, its croak blending with the whisper of the trees along the river's edge. Jonah listened, feeling as if he were lying under a canopy of trees, with leaves dancing above him in the soft glow of moonlight.

The trees along the river swayed in time with the frog's lullaby, their branches forming gentle arches that seemed to hug the river, creating a cozy, hidden path. Jonah could almost feel the cool, earthy scent of the forest wrapping around him, filling his heart with a sense of peace.

"Thank you, Mr. Frog," Jonah said, smiling as he drifted past the green waters. The frog gave him a little wave, hopping back onto his lily pad as Jonah continued downstream.

As the river curved, the green faded, and the water began to glow with a soft, golden light. Jonah's heart lifted as he saw tiny flickers of light dancing along the riverbanks—fireflies, glowing like stars, their soft light casting a warm, golden hue over everything.

The river was now filled with a soft yellow glow, like sunlight on a quiet morning. The fireflies twinkled and danced around Jonah, filling the air with a warm, sleepy feeling, like the first rays of dawn.

One of the fireflies landed on his shoulder, its tiny light flickering gently. "Welcome to the yellow part of the river," it whispered. "Here, we bring dreams of warmth and light, of cozy mornings and the soft glow of sunrise."

Jonah closed his eyes, letting the gentle warmth of the fireflies fill him with a feeling of safety and comfort. He imagined himself wrapped in the light of a morning sun, surrounded by the gentle hum of fireflies as they welcomed a new day.

With a soft sigh of gratitude, Jonah opened his eyes and watched as the river began to change color again, shifting from warm yellow to a soft, dreamy pink.

The pink part of the river sparkled with a delicate, rose-colored glow, and as Jonah drifted into it, he noticed beautiful butterflies fluttering all around him. Their wings shimmered with shades of pink and purple, each one trailing tiny specks of stardust as they floated gracefully through the air.

One of the butterflies landed lightly on his hand, its wings moving slowly, like a gentle heartbeat. "Welcome to the pink part of the river, Jonah," it said softly. "Here, we bring dreams of wonder and adventure, of magical places and starlit skies."

Jonah felt his heart fill with excitement, a spark of wonder lighting up inside him. The butterflies flitted around him, creating soft patterns of light in the air. He imagined himself exploring enchanted forests, discovering secret paths and hidden worlds, all bathed in the soft glow of starlight.

"Thank you, little butterfly," Jonah whispered, his voice filled with awe. The butterfly gave a tiny nod, lifting off his hand and rejoining the others as they drifted through the pink light.

As the river flowed on, the pink glow began to deepen into a rich, soothing purple. The air was filled with the scent of lavender, and Jonah felt his eyelids growing heavier, lulled by the peaceful calm of the purple waters.

In the purple part of the river, Jonah saw tiny stars floating along the surface, each one casting a soft, silvery light. The stars seemed to hum a gentle lullaby, filling the air with a melody that made him feel as if he were wrapped in a cozy blanket.

A small, wise-looking owl perched on a branch overhanging the river, watching him with kind, sleepy eyes. "Welcome to the purple part of the river, Jonah," the owl said in a soft, soothing voice. "Here, we bring dreams of rest and peace, of quiet nights and the gentle embrace of sleep."

The owl began to hum along with the stars, its voice blending into the lullaby. Jonah felt his body relax, sinking deeper into the soft warmth of the lily pad. He closed his eyes, letting the owl's lullaby wrap around him like a gentle hug.

"Thank you, Mr. Owl," Jonah murmured, his voice barely more than a whisper. The owl gave him a slow, sleepy nod, continuing its song as Jonah drifted past.

As he floated further downstream, the colors of the

river began to blend together, creating a soft, shimmering rainbow of light. Each color held a piece of the dreams he had experienced—blue for the calming waves, green for the peaceful forests, yellow for warmth and light, pink for wonder, and purple for rest.

The lily pad began to slow, gently guiding Jonah back toward his room. The rainbow colors surrounded him, filling his heart with warmth and peace, as if he were carrying a piece of each dream with him.

Before he knew it, he was back in his room, lying in his bed. The colorful river slowly faded, but its warmth remained, wrapping around him like a cozy blanket. Jonah closed his eyes, feeling the gentle glow of the rainbow dreams filling his mind.

As he drifted into a deep, peaceful sleep, he dreamed of the River of Rainbow Dreams, with its gentle dolphins, sleepy frogs, dancing fireflies, magical butterflies, and wise owls. Each dream was a reminder of the journey he had taken, a journey through colors and warmth, through peace and wonder.

And from that night on, whenever Jonah closed his eyes, he knew the River of Rainbow Dreams would be waiting for him, a magical place where colors came to life, filling his heart with joy, peace, and the beauty of dreams.

# The Enchanted Bedtime Library

Max loved books. He loved the way they smelled, the way the pages crinkled softly as he turned them, and most of all, he loved the worlds they held within them. The library was his favorite place in the whole world. Every time he visited, he felt like an explorer, uncovering new stories and adventures hidden among the shelves.

One quiet evening, as the sun dipped below the horizon and the library grew dim, Max was wandering the aisles, running his fingers over the rows of books, feeling the magic that each one held. Just as he was about to head back to the main entrance, something unusual caught his eye. At the very end of the last row of shelves, half-hidden in shadows, was a small door.

He hadn't noticed it before, and he felt a thrill of curiosity.

Without thinking twice, he walked toward the door, gently nudging it open. It creaked softly, and Max stepped inside, finding himself in a cozy room that looked like a miniature library of its own. Soft, golden light filled the room, coming from books that glowed gently on the shelves, casting a warm, calming glow that made Max feel immediately at ease.

"Hello there," came a soft, friendly voice from above.

Max looked up and gasped in surprise. Perched on a small, polished bookstand was an owl—a tiny, wise-looking creature with big, round eyes, soft feathers the color of aged parchment, and a pair of little spectacles resting on the tip of its beak.

"Good evening, young reader," the owl said, bowing slightly. "I'm Scribbles, the librarian of the Enchanted Bedtime Library. Welcome."

Max's eyes sparkled with excitement. "The Enchanted Bedtime Library?"

"Yes, indeed," Scribbles replied, adjusting his spectacles with one wing. "This library is very special. Here, every book holds a magical story meant to come alive in dreams. Every evening, the Enchanted Bedtime

Library opens its doors to those who love stories deeply."

Max's heart swelled with joy. "I do love stories! Can you show me around?"

Scribbles gave a warm, approving nod and fluttered down from his bookstand, landing softly on Max's shoulder. "It would be my pleasure. Follow me, Max."

As they wandered through the Enchanted Bedtime Library, Max noticed that each book was unique, with intricate covers that seemed to shimmer in the soft light. Some books floated down from the shelves on their own, gently opening to show glimpses of enchanted forests, glowing under the light of a silver moon. Others whispered soft melodies, their covers painted with stars and distant kingdoms.

"Every book here has its own special world," Scribbles explained. "These books are written by the dreams and wishes of every child who has ever dreamed of a story, a magical place, or a grand adventure."

Max was captivated. He watched in awe as one book opened to reveal a gentle river flowing through a misty forest, where fireflies danced like stars. Another book showed a castle made of starlight, perched high on a cloud, where a princess sat reading by a window that overlooked the sky.

"Can I pick a book to read?" Max asked, his voice barely more than a whisper.

Scribbles smiled, his eyes twinkling. "Of course. But first, let's meet a few of the stories who've been waiting patiently for a reader to come along."

They came to a shelf where a little book with a cover of green leaves floated down and opened up, revealing a scene of a hidden glen surrounded by ancient, wise trees. The trees had faces carved into their bark, and their eyes seemed to sparkle with kindness. In the middle of the glen, a tiny unicorn with a mane made of dandelion fluff pranced around, spreading gentle wishes and laughter.

"This is *The Forest of Gentle Dreams,*" Scribbles said softly. "Anyone who reads this book will find themselves in a peaceful forest where every tree has a story, and every leaf has a whisper of kindness to share. It's a place of calm and wonder."

Max smiled, feeling a soft warmth spreading through him. He felt as if he could hear the trees, their voices low and soothing, telling tales of the forest and its many secrets.

They continued to the next shelf, where a book with a deep blue cover floated down and opened. Inside, Max saw a vast, starry sky filled with glowing constellations and soft, fluffy clouds. A tiny fox with a coat that shimmered like silver stardust wandered across the sky, occasionally stopping to chase a shooting star.

"This one is called *The Starry Night Stroll*," Scribbles explained. "It takes readers on a journey through a world of stars and constellations, led by a wise little fox who knows the paths through the night sky. Readers find themselves surrounded by peaceful starlight, each star carrying a lullaby for gentle dreams."

Max could almost hear the soft hum of the stars and feel the quiet calm of a nighttime sky. He looked at Scribbles, his heart full of excitement and wonder. "I want to read all of them!" he whispered.

Scribbles chuckled, his feathers fluffing up in delight. "In time, dear Max. Tonight, I have a special book in mind, just for you."

With a flap of his wings, Scribbles led Max to a cozy armchair in the corner of the library. He gestured to a nearby shelf, and a book with a cover painted in shades of gold and soft lavender floated down. The book settled gently into Max's hands, and he felt a warm glow radiating from it.

"This is *The Tale of Bravery and Kindness*," Scribbles said with a gentle smile. "It's a story meant for dreamers like you, filled with gentle adventures and the magic of kindness. This book will guide you through a world where courage and warmth light the way."

Max opened the book, his eyes widening as the pages came to life under his fingertips. Inside, he saw a meadow bathed in the golden light of dawn, where tiny, friendly creatures wandered peacefully. Rabbits with soft, velvety fur hopped through the grass, birds with shimmering feathers sang gentle melodies, and a little hedgehog offered Max a flower as a welcome gift.

The words of the story began to whisper to him, each sentence filling his heart with a calm, cozy warmth. He felt as if he were truly in the meadow, surrounded by the gentle creatures who greeted him with kindness and warmth.

As he turned the pages, the story took him on a journey through quiet forests, where the trees whispered words of encouragement, and past streams where fireflies danced in soft patterns, casting tiny lights that seemed to spell out words of friendship.

"Each book in this library has the power to make you feel as if you're really there," Scribbles said softly. "As you read, you'll find yourself carried along by the story, surrounded by the world within its pages."

Max felt his eyelids growing heavy, the gentle words of the story wrapping around him like a blanket. The glow from the book filled the air with a soft, golden light, making him feel as if he were floating in a dream.

He continued reading, the book guiding him to a starlit garden filled with flowers that glowed with a soft, silvery light. The flowers seemed to hum a lullaby, their petals swaying gently in the moonlight. Max felt a deep sense of calm wash over him, as if the story itself were holding him close, keeping him safe and warm.

As he reached the final pages, he saw a scene of a little village bathed in the soft light of dawn, where all the animals were tucked snugly into their cozy homes, sleeping peacefully as the morning light began to rise.

The book whispered a final line to him, as gentle as a sigh. "In this world of kindness and dreams, courage and warmth fill every heart, and peace is a promise carried on the wind."

Max closed the book, a smile on his face and his heart filled with joy. He looked at Scribbles, his eyes sleepy but filled with gratitude. "Thank you, Scribbles," he murmured. "This was the best story I've ever read."

Scribbles gave him a warm, wise nod. "You are always welcome in the Enchanted Bedtime Library, Max. Remember, these stories are here for you whenever you need a place of peace and warmth."

With a soft flap of his wings, Scribbles gestured

toward the door, and Max felt himself becoming lighter, as if he were floating. The cozy warmth of the library began to blur, the soft glow of the books casting a gentle light as the world around him grew hazy.

When Max opened his eyes, he was back in his room, snuggled under his blankets. The memory of the Enchanted Bedtime Library filled him with a quiet peace, as if he could still feel the soft glow of the magical books and hear the gentle hum of the stories.

As he closed his eyes, he knew he would dream of the magical worlds he had explored with Scribbles, of starlit gardens and glowing meadows, and of the cozy, welcoming warmth of the Enchanted Bedtime Library.

And from that night on, every time he opened a book, he felt the magic of the library with him, as if each story held a doorway to a place of gentle dreams, waiting to carry him off into a world of peace and wonder.

# The Firefly's Secret Lantern Festival

Lily loved summer nights. She especially loved the fireflies that filled her backyard as the sun dipped below the horizon. Every evening, she'd sit by the window or lie in the grass, watching them blink and sparkle, dancing like tiny stars come down to Earth. She imagined they had their own secret world, where they lived in tiny glowing houses and had little firefly parties after dark.

One warm evening, just as dusk was falling, Lily noticed one firefly that was brighter than all the rest. Its light glowed with a golden warmth, a bit like a tiny lantern. She watched, captivated, as it blinked, then blinked again, as if calling her over.

*Is it trying to tell me something?* she wondered.

With curiosity bubbling up inside her, Lily got up and quietly followed the bright little firefly. It hovered at the edge of the woods near her backyard, and as she approached, it drifted deeper into the trees, its light blinking steadily to guide her. She tiptoed along the path, feeling like she was on a secret adventure, the kind she had only read about in books.

After following the glow through the trees for what felt like forever, she finally stepped into a hidden meadow. And there, she saw something that took her breath away: the entire meadow was filled with fireflies, thousands of them glowing and floating, filling the air with soft light. They looked like stars come down from the sky, each one casting a gentle glow that made the meadow feel like a magical world.

"Welcome, Lily!" a cheerful little voice chimed.

Startled, Lily looked around to find the source of the voice. The bright firefly that had led her to the meadow was now hovering right in front of her, glowing even brighter than before.

"My name is Flick," the firefly said, his voice warm and friendly. "And I brought you here because tonight is a very special night. You've been invited to the annual Firefly Lantern Festival!"

"The Firefly Lantern Festival?" Lily whispered, her

eyes wide with wonder. She had never heard of such a thing, but it sounded magical.

Flick nodded, his light blinking excitedly. "Yes! Every summer, we fireflies gather to celebrate light and share peaceful dreams with all the children who watch us. It's the biggest, coziest light show of the year. We've been preparing all week!"

Lily's heart filled with excitement. She had always loved watching the fireflies in her yard, but she had never imagined they held a festival of their own. She felt like she had stumbled into a secret world, one that only fireflies knew about.

"Come along," Flick said, buzzing ahead. "There's much to do before the festival begins!"

Lily followed Flick through the meadow, her heart racing with excitement. The meadow was filled with tiny flowers, tall grasses, and delicate tree branches, and everywhere she looked, fireflies were flitting about, hanging tiny lanterns made of dewdrops and gossamer threads. Each lantern glowed with a soft, magical light, casting a warm glow over the meadow that made it feel like a dream.

"Would you like to help us hang lanterns?" Flick asked, his voice filled with kindness.

Lily nodded eagerly, her face lighting up with joy.

She carefully took a tiny lantern that Flick handed her, marveling at how light and delicate it felt. She tiptoed over to a tall blade of grass and gently hung the lantern on it, watching as it swayed in the gentle breeze, casting a soft glow over the ground below.

As she hung more lanterns, Lily noticed the other fireflies buzzing around her, each one glowing in different shades of yellow, gold, and even a soft pink. They worked together in harmony, hanging lanterns on flowers, grasses, and tree branches, turning the meadow into a shimmering wonderland. The entire place seemed to glow with warmth and magic, like a starry sky on Earth.

"Beautiful work, Lily!" Flick said with a proud little buzz. "You're a natural at this."

Lily beamed, her heart swelling with happiness. She felt like she was part of something truly special, something magical that only happened in the quietest corners of the world.

As the last lanterns were hung, the fireflies gathered together in the center of the meadow. Flick turned to Lily, his eyes twinkling with excitement. "And now, it's time for the festival dance!"

The fireflies began to swirl and dance, their lights blinking in patterns that filled the meadow with a gentle, calming rhythm. Some flew in circles, others in soft loops, creating waves of light that washed over the meadow like ripples in a pond. As Lily watched, she felt as though she were floating among the stars, drifting through a sea of gentle light.

Flick joined the dance, spiraling around Lily in graceful loops. "We dance to share our light," he explained, his voice filled with pride. "Every blink and every glow is a wish for warmth, peace, and happy dreams for all who see us."

Lily closed her eyes, letting the gentle light fill her heart with calm. She could feel the wishes of the fireflies wrapping around her like a warm, cozy blanket, filling her with a sense of peace and contentment. The soft hum of their wings created a lullaby that made her feel drowsy, as if the whole world were inviting her to sleep.

As the dance continued, the fireflies formed a circle around Lily, their lights blinking softly in a rhythm that made her feel as though she were in a cradle of warmth and light. The gentle, pulsing glow lulled her into a peaceful state, her eyelids growing heavy with each blink of light.

"Thank you for joining us, Lily," Flick whispered, his voice soft and kind. "The festival wouldn't be the same without you."

Lily smiled sleepily, feeling a wave of gratitude

wash over her. "Thank you, Flick," she murmured, her voice barely more than a whisper. "This has been the most magical night of my life."

Flick gave a little bow, his tiny wings fluttering. "We'll always be here, dancing and sharing our light. Anytime you need peaceful dreams, just look for our glow, and we'll be here."

With that, the fireflies drifted closer, their gentle glow surrounding her like a warm, comforting hug. The meadow grew softer, quieter, as if the world itself were settling down to sleep. Lily felt Flick's warm light guiding her, wrapping her in a blanket of calm as she drifted into slumber.

In her dreams, she floated through the glowing meadow, surrounded by the gentle, blinking lights of her firefly friends. She could feel their warmth, their wishes for peace and happiness, filling her heart with a joy she had never felt before.

When Lily opened her eyes, she was back in her bed, wrapped snugly in her blanket. The morning sun was peeking through her window, casting a warm light over her room. But as she lay there, she could still feel the gentle glow of the fireflies and the warmth of the magical meadow in her heart.

From that day on, every time she saw a firefly, Lily felt a sense of peace, knowing that Flick and the other fireflies were out there, sharing their light and wishes with the world. And on warm summer nights, she would lie in her yard, watching the fireflies dance, and remember the magical night of the Firefly Lantern Festival.

# The Sleepy Island of Shimmering Shells

Toby loved the ocean. He loved its waves, its endless shades of blue, and the mystery of what lay beneath its shimmering surface. Every summer, his family would take a trip to the beach, and Toby would spend hours collecting shells, imagining that each one was a treasure from a magical underwater world. He often dreamed of going on an adventure under the sea, exploring hidden coves, and discovering creatures who called the ocean their home.

One night, as Toby climbed into bed, he found something unusual under his pillow. It was a seashell—one he had never seen before. It was small, round, and glowed with a soft, pastel light that seemed to pulse gently, like a heartbeat. Intrigued, he picked it up, noticing a tiny note tucked inside.

The note read: "Dear Toby, you're invited to the Sleepy Island of Shimmering Shells. Close your eyes, hold this shell, and let it guide you to a place of peace and dreams."

With his heart full of excitement, Toby did exactly as the note instructed. He clutched the shell in his hand, closed his eyes, and took a deep breath. Almost immediately, he felt a gentle, swaying sensation, like he was floating on water.

When he opened his eyes, Toby found himself standing on the softest, whitest sand he'd ever seen. Gentle waves lapped at the shore, and the entire island seemed to glow under a sky filled with stars. Everywhere he looked, he saw seashells of every shape and color scattered across the sand. Each shell emitted a soft, pastel light—pink, blue, lavender, and mint—casting a peaceful glow over the beach. The shells sang gentle lullabies, their tiny, tinkling voices blending with the sound of the waves, creating a melody that made Toby feel calm and safe.

As he gazed around in wonder, a large, gentle sea turtle emerged from the waves. She had a wise, kind face, and her shell glimmered with soft, glowing patterns like the shells on the beach. She moved with a slow, graceful rhythm, as though she had all the time in the world.

"Welcome to the Sleepy Island of Shimmering Shells, Toby," the turtle said in a warm, soothing voice. "My name is Coral, and I am the keeper of this island."

Toby smiled, feeling instantly at ease. "Hi, Coral," he replied, his voice filled with excitement. "This place is amazing! I've never seen anything like it."

Coral nodded, her wise eyes twinkling. "This island is a place of peace and dreams. Here, every shell holds a gentle memory of the sea, collected from the waves that travel across the world. Would you like me to show you around?"

Toby's heart filled with joy. "Yes, please!"

Coral led him along a path made entirely of glowing shells, each one humming a soft, calming tune as he stepped on it. The shells felt warm and smooth beneath his bare feet, and the melody they played made him feel as if he were walking through a dream.

Their first stop was a shimmering lagoon nestled in a cove. The water was perfectly still, glowing with a gentle blue light. As Toby looked closer, he noticed dozens of tiny, glowing fish swimming slowly in circles. Their scales sparkled like diamonds, and they moved with a graceful rhythm, almost like a dance.

"These are the Dreamfish," Coral explained, her voice a soothing murmur. "They swim in endless circles, creating ripples of peace and calm. Every ripple carries a gentle dream, which floats across the lagoon and settles over the island."

Toby watched the Dreamfish, feeling a sense of quiet happiness fill him. He could almost see the dreams they were sending out—soft images of moonlit seas, calm waves, and starlit skies. The gentle rhythm of their movements made him feel as if he were floating, as light as a feather.

Coral guided him further along the beach, where the shells glowed in soft, cool colors. The breeze picked up, rustling the palms and grasses, and Toby realized the wind was more than just a breeze—it was a voice, whispering secrets from the sea.

"Listen carefully, Toby," Coral said, her wise eyes sparkling. "The breeze here carries stories from the ocean, tales collected from every wave that has touched these shores."

Toby closed his eyes and listened. The breeze whispered soft words, telling him of distant lands where coral reefs glowed under the moonlight, of whales that sang songs to the stars, and of hidden underwater caves where seashells shimmered like precious gems.

The breeze's stories filled Toby's mind with images of endless blue waters, mysterious sea creatures, and worlds hidden beneath the waves. Each story seemed to wrap around him, as comforting as a warm blanket, making him feel safe and content.

They continued along the path, and Coral led him to a small, round pool surrounded by shells that glowed in shades of pink and lavender. The water in the pool was still and clear, and Toby noticed that there were tiny bubbles floating up from the depths, each one glowing softly.

"These are Dream Bubbles," Coral said with a gentle smile. "Each bubble holds a quiet, calming dream, like the gentle rise and fall of the ocean. When the bubbles reach the surface, the dreams drift up into the sky and travel to children all over the world, bringing peaceful sleep."

Toby watched as a bubble rose slowly, its glow casting a soft light over his face. It burst gently at the surface, sending a warm wave of peace washing over him. He felt a cozy warmth settle in his chest, like the feeling he got when he snuggled into bed on a chilly night.

Coral leaned down and gave him a gentle nudge with her nose. "Would you like to collect some shells to take home, Toby? Each one holds a lullaby from the ocean, a song of calm that will help you drift off to sleep whenever you need it."

Toby's face lit up with joy. "I'd love that!"

He began gathering shells, carefully selecting ones that glowed softly in shades of blue, pink, and green. Each shell felt warm in his hand, humming with a gentle melody that made him feel drowsy and content. As he held them, he imagined himself floating on a calm sea, surrounded by the glowing shells of the Sleepy Island.

When he had collected a handful of shells, Coral led him back to the spot where they had started. The island was quiet now, bathed in the gentle glow of the shells and the soft, twinkling light of stars overhead.

"It's time for you to return home, Toby," Coral said softly. "But don't worry. The magic of the Sleepy Island will always be with you, in every shell you carry."

Toby nodded, feeling a mixture of happiness and sleepiness. "Thank you, Coral. This has been the best adventure ever."

Coral gave him a warm, wise smile. "Goodnight, Toby. May the ocean's dreams bring you peace and comfort."

With those words, Toby felt himself becoming lighter, as if he were floating on a soft wave. The island around him began to blur, and he closed his eyes, letting the gentle lullabies of the shells fill his heart.

When he opened his eyes again, he was back in his

room, nestled under his blanket. In his hand, he still held one of the glowing shells, its soft light casting a warm glow over his room. He placed it under his pillow, feeling the gentle hum of the ocean's lullaby as he closed his eyes.

That night, Toby dreamed of the Sleepy Island of Shimmering Shells. He dreamed of glowing beaches, peaceful lagoons, and a wise sea turtle named Coral. The lullabies of the shells filled his dreams with calm, carrying him on gentle waves to a place of warmth and peace.

And every night after, whenever he needed a little extra comfort, Toby would slip the shell under his pillow, letting the magic of the Sleepy Island fill his heart and lull him into the coziest, most peaceful sleep.

# The Star Sheep of Midnight Meadows

In a quiet, sleepy countryside, twelve-year-old Sophie often lay in bed at night, gazing out her window at the stars. She loved watching them twinkle and sparkle, imagining they were her silent, watchful friends. She would whisper her secrets to them, trusting that the stars would keep them safe, drifting far beyond anyone's reach.

One evening, as Sophie was about to close her eyes, she noticed something unusual. The stars seemed lower, closer to the Earth, and their glow was warmer than usual, like tiny cozy nightlights scattered across the sky. Curiosity got the best of her, and with a quiet thrill of adventure, she slipped out of bed, threw on her slippers, and tiptoed down the stairs and out of the house, heading toward the open fields.

She made her way across the moonlit countryside, following the soft, silvery glow that seemed to pull her forward. After a short walk, Sophie reached a meadow she had never seen before, a place where the grass glistened under a blanket of stars. But these weren't just any stars—these stars were gathered in the form of fluffy, glowing sheep.

Sophie's eyes widened in wonder as she took in the sight of the magical meadow. The sheep were luminous, their wool glowing in gentle hues of white, silver, and even pale shades of blue and lavender. Each one glowed softly, casting a cozy light that made the whole meadow look like a dream.

"Welcome to Midnight Meadows," came a warm, gentle voice from behind her.

Sophie turned and saw a tall figure dressed in flowing midnight-blue robes, his face kind and his eyes twinkling like stars. He held a long staff with a crescent moon at the top, which glowed faintly in the night.

"My name is Orion, the Star Shepherd," the man said, smiling at her. "Every night, I guide the Star Sheep to graze here on the meadow's stardust-covered grass, so they can shine brightly when they return to the sky."

Sophie's heart filled with excitement and wonder.

"Are they really stars?" she asked in a hushed, awe-filled voice.

Orion nodded. "Yes, they are. During the day, they rest in the heavens, but each night, they come down to Midnight Meadows to recharge their light by grazing on stardust. And tonight, I could use a bit of help. Would you like to join me in guiding the Star Sheep?"

Sophie beamed with joy. "I'd love to!"

Orion handed her a small, glowing lantern. "Hold this high as we walk. The light will help us keep the Star Sheep together. You'll also need to count them so we know none get left behind."

As they strolled into the meadow, Sophie noticed the soft hum of the Star Sheep's breathing, like a lullaby that filled the air. She lifted her lantern and counted the sheep nearby. There were dozens scattered around, each one glowing with a soft, cozy light that made her feel warm and peaceful.

They walked along, and Orion showed her how to guide the sheep gently, coaxing them together with the soft glow of the lantern. As they moved, Sophie realized that each sheep's light felt different, almost like it carried a special warmth.

"This one," Orion said, pointing to a sheep with a particularly warm glow, "is Dreamy. His light is filled with peaceful dreams, the kind that make you feel safe and snug."

Sophie reached out to pet Dreamy, feeling his soft wool, which was like touching a cloud. A gentle calm washed over her, making her feel drowsy and content. She noticed another Star Sheep, a little one with a delicate lavender glow.

"That's Sparkle," Orion said with a smile. "Sparkle's light brings a cheerful warmth. When children see her, they feel happy and loved."

Sophie knelt down and let Sparkle nuzzle her hand, and a joyful, cozy feeling filled her heart, like she was wrapped in a hug. As they walked along, she met several other Star Sheep, each one giving her a different, comforting feeling. Some made her feel calm, others filled her with warmth, and all of them made her feel as if she were wrapped in a soft, glowing blanket of light.

As the night went on, Orion taught her how to gently count each Star Sheep, guiding them back together as they grazed. "Counting sheep helps keep them close," he explained. "And as you count them, you'll find a peaceful rhythm, one that helps lull you to sleep."

Sophie counted each sheep softly, her voice a whisper in the quiet meadow. "One... two... three..."

With each count, she felt her own eyelids growing heavier, the warmth of the Star Sheep's light surrounding her like a cozy blanket.

They continued walking through the meadow, gathering all the sheep in a gentle circle under a large, old oak tree. The tree's branches stretched high into the night sky, and its leaves sparkled faintly, as if catching some of the light from the sheep below. Sophie noticed one of the Star Sheep—a slightly larger one with a soft, golden glow—gazing up at the tree with wise, twinkling eyes.

"That's Elder," Orion said with a smile. "He's the oldest of the Star Sheep, and he watches over the others, helping them find their way back to the sky."

Sophie gave Elder a gentle pat on his soft wool, feeling his warmth radiate like a cozy fire on a chilly night. The Star Sheep around her began to settle down, each one curling up on the soft grass, their lights dimming as they nestled close together.

Orion looked at Sophie, his eyes warm with gratitude. "Thank you for helping us tonight, Sophie. You've done a wonderful job keeping the Star Sheep together."

Sophie smiled sleepily, her heart full of joy. "Thank you for letting me help, Orion. This has been the most magical night of my life."

Orion nodded, placing a gentle hand on her shoulder. "The magic of Midnight Meadows is always here, Sophie, and the Star Sheep will always be watching over you, filling the night sky with warmth and peace. Whenever you need comfort, just look up at the stars, and know that they're there, shining just for you."

As the last of the Star Sheep began to drift up toward the sky, each one's glow fading as it rose, Orion gave Sophie a gentle hug, filling her with a final wave of warmth and calm. She closed her eyes, feeling the magic of the meadow wrapping around her like a soft blanket.

When she opened her eyes, she was back in her bed, the faintest glow of starlight shining through her window. She nestled into her pillow, her heart full of peaceful, happy memories of the Star Sheep and Midnight Meadows.

And as she drifted into sleep, she dreamed of cozy, glowing fields and fluffy friends, of a wise Star Shepherd named Orion, and the gentle, glowing Star Sheep who filled the night sky with dreams and light.

# The Dreamboat Voyage to Cloud Island

Jack and Lisa were best friends who shared everything —books, snacks, and even grand adventures in their backyard. But they had never been on a nighttime adventure. Every evening, as they said goodbye, they would imagine what it would be like to fly through the starry sky, touching the clouds and visiting distant, magical lands.

One warm evening, as they were saying goodnight, Jack noticed something unusual just outside his bedroom window. It looked like a small boat, but not just any boat—it was covered in fluffy white clouds, with sails that looked as soft as marshmallows, glowing with a soft, silvery light like the moon.

"Lisa, look!" he whispered excitedly, leaning out

his window. Lisa leaned out of her own window next door and gasped when she saw the boat. The little vessel bobbed gently in the air, as if waiting for them.

They quickly tiptoed out of bed and hurried to the strange, magical boat floating outside. Tied to the mast was a tiny note that glowed softly in the night. It read: "Welcome aboard the Dreamboat! Next stop: Cloud Island!"

Jack and Lisa looked at each other with wide eyes and huge grins. They didn't need to say a word—they knew this was the adventure they had always dreamed of.

Climbing carefully into the Dreamboat, they found that the seats were soft and warm, like a cloud had wrapped itself around them. As soon as they were settled, the Dreamboat began to rise, gently floating higher and higher into the night sky, carried by a breeze that felt as soft as a whisper. The stars twinkled above them, and the world below looked like a patchwork quilt of sleepy houses and twinkling streetlights.

The boat sailed quietly through the sky, leaving a trail of silvery mist behind. Jack and Lisa leaned over the side, watching the clouds drift by, each one glowing faintly under the starlight. The air smelled sweet, like fresh rain and the scent of blooming flowers.

As they floated along, a soft splashing sound caught their attention. Just below the Dreamboat, they saw a shape rising up from the mist—a cloud dolphin, glistening and glowing as if made from pure stardust. The dolphin had a friendly smile and sparkling eyes that twinkled like stars.

"Hello there!" the dolphin greeted them in a cheerful voice. "I'm Fluffy, your guide to Cloud Island! I'll be leading the way!"

Jack and Lisa clapped their hands with excitement. "Hi, Fluffy! We're Jack and Lisa. We've never met a cloud dolphin before!" Lisa said, her voice full of wonder.

Fluffy gave a playful twirl in the air, sending soft rings of mist around them. "It's my pleasure to meet you both! Cloud Island is a magical place where dreams are created, shaped by cloud creatures who fill the night with peace and wonder. You'll love it!"

The Dreamboat continued its gentle voyage, with Fluffy diving and leaping alongside, creating misty hoops that shimmered in the moonlight. Jack and Lisa laughed, reaching out to touch the mist, which felt cool and soft, like touching a cloud.

Before long, a glimmering land appeared in the distance. It looked like an island floating in the sky, covered in billowy clouds that sparkled with hues of blue, pink, and lavender. Small, fluffy creatures were bouncing and floating all over, each one glowing softly. As they got closer, Jack and Lisa could see that the island was filled with cloud animals—little cloud bunnies, gentle cloud bears, and even a cloud lion with a mane that rippled like a soft breeze.

"Welcome to Cloud Island!" Fluffy announced with a cheerful whistle as the Dreamboat drifted gently to a stop on a soft cloud shore.

Jack and Lisa stepped off the Dreamboat, their feet sinking into the soft, pillowy ground. The cloud creatures gathered around them, their eyes twinkling with warmth and welcome.

A round, fluffy cloud bear waddled over and gave them a gentle nuzzle. "Hello, children! I'm Puffy, one of the dream weavers here on Cloud Island," he said in a soft, calming voice. "We're so happy to have you here. Tonight, we're creating dreams for all the children below, and we could use a little help."

Jack and Lisa's eyes sparkled with excitement. "We'd love to help!" Jack replied eagerly.

Puffy led them along a path of glowing cloud flowers, each one humming with a soft melody. "Dreams are woven here on Cloud Island every night," he explained. "The cloud creatures help shape the dreams, filling them with gentle wonders to bring peace and happiness to everyone sleeping below."

Their first stop was a grove of fluffy, rainbow-colored trees that gently swayed in a soft breeze. Underneath the trees, several cloud bunnies were hopping around, collecting handfuls of stardust in little pouches made of clouds. Each time the bunnies sprinkled a handful of stardust over the ground, beautiful images would appear—a glowing forest, a sparkling ocean, or a field of twinkling flowers.

"Would you like to help sprinkle some stardust?" a tiny cloud bunny asked, hopping up to Lisa with a pouch full of shimmering dust.

"Oh, yes, please!" Lisa exclaimed. She took a handful of stardust, feeling its cool, soft shimmer in her hand, and scattered it gently over the clouds. As the stardust fell, a scene of an enchanted forest appeared, with trees glowing in shades of green and blue, each one filled with tiny, twinkling fireflies.

Jack watched in awe, then eagerly reached for some stardust of his own. As he sprinkled it, a cozy castle appeared, its towers glowing under a silver moon, with fluffy clouds billowing from the windows like soft smoke.

Puffy smiled, his big cloud eyes twinkling. "Wonderful work, Jack and Lisa! These scenes will be woven into dreams for children all over the world, bringing them peaceful and happy dreams."

The two friends felt a warm glow in their hearts, knowing they were helping create beautiful dreams for others. They continued along the path with Puffy, their footsteps making little puffs of mist with every step.

Next, they arrived at a sparkling lagoon where tiny, glowing fish floated lazily in the cloud water, their scales shimmering like tiny stars. A group of cloud dolphins, smaller than Fluffy, leaped gently through the water, leaving trails of soft light behind them.

"These are the Dreamfish," Puffy explained. "They swim through dreams, bringing a feeling of calm and peace to those who see them."

Jack and Lisa knelt by the lagoon, watching the Dreamfish as they swirled in graceful circles, their tiny lights reflecting off the misty water. The sight was so peaceful that they felt their own eyes grow a little heavier, a gentle sleepiness settling over them.

As they continued exploring Cloud Island, they came upon a small grove where a group of cloud creatures was gathered, shaping tiny clouds into soft shapes. Some clouds became pillows, others formed into cozy blankets, each one glowing softly as it was placed onto a fluffy bed made of moonlight.

"These are the Dream Beds," Puffy explained. "Every night, we make these to carry dreams down to the children below. Each bed is filled with warmth, comfort, and peaceful dreams."

The cloud animals worked together, weaving gentle lullabies into the Dream Beds as they worked. Lisa and Jack helped fluff the little cloud pillows, adding sprinkles of stardust here and there, watching as the pillows glowed with a soft, warm light.

They continued to help until all the Dream Beds were ready, each one glowing softly, filled with cozy dreams that would drift down to the children below. As they looked around, they realized that the entire island was aglow with warmth, a peaceful light filling every corner.

Fluffy, the cloud dolphin, swam over, gliding through the air with his friendly smile. "You two have been such wonderful helpers," he said, looping gracefully around them. "It's almost time for the Dream-boat to take you home, but first, we have a little gift."

Puffy handed each of them a tiny, fluffy cloud, soft and glowing with a gentle light. "Keep these beside your beds," he said with a kind smile. "Whenever you need a peaceful sleep, just hold them close, and they'll remind you of your time on Cloud Island."

Jack and Lisa held the little clouds close, feeling the

warmth and peace radiating from them. "Thank you so much, Puffy and Fluffy," Jack said, his voice filled with gratitude.

"It's been the best adventure," Lisa added, smiling sleepily.

The Dreamboat was waiting for them, its cloud sails billowing softly in the breeze. They climbed aboard, snuggling into the cozy seats, each holding their tiny cloud close. As the Dreamboat lifted gently into the sky, they looked back at Cloud Island, watching as the cloud creatures waved goodbye, their soft glow lighting up the island like a constellation in the sky.

The Dreamboat drifted peacefully through the night, the stars twinkling above them, the gentle sound of the wind a lullaby in their ears. Jack and Lisa leaned back, feeling their eyes grow heavier and heavier, their hearts full of the warmth and joy of the magical island they had just visited.

As the Dreamboat floated down and settled outside their windows, Jack and Lisa quietly climbed back into their rooms, placing the tiny glowing clouds beside their beds. They snuggled under their blankets, feeling as if they were still on the Dreamboat, floating among the stars.

That night, they dreamed of Cloud Island, of the

fluffy, glowing friends they had made, of sprinkling stardust and creating beautiful dreams. And every night after, whenever they held their little clouds close, they felt a wave of peace and warmth, knowing that Cloud Island was always there, waiting for their next adventure.

# The Cozy Cave of Dreams

One quiet night, as a gentle breeze whispered through the trees, twins Luke and Lila lay snuggled in their beds, sound asleep. The world was wrapped in the calm of midnight, the stars twinkling above like tiny lights in the sky. But as they dreamed, a soft sound drifted into their room—a gentle "hoot-hoo, hoot-hoo," as if calling to them.

Lila opened her eyes first, blinking sleepily, and saw a tiny owl perched on their windowsill. The owl's feathers were a soft shade of brown, with a touch of silver that shimmered in the moonlight, and her eyes were wide and friendly.

"Hello, Luke and Lila," the little owl said in a voice as gentle as a lullaby. "My name is Tilly. I've come to invite you to a very special place—the Cozy Cave of Dreams."

At the sound of her voice, Luke opened his eyes, too, his curiosity piqued. "The Cozy Cave of Dreams?" he whispered, sitting up in bed.

Tilly nodded, her eyes twinkling with warmth. "Yes, it's a magical cave in the enchanted mountains, where sleepy animals and tired travelers go to find rest. Would you like to visit?"

Luke and Lila looked at each other, their eyes shining with excitement. They both loved adventure, and the idea of visiting a secret cave sounded wonderful. "We'd love to!" they said together.

Tilly fluffed her feathers, clearly delighted. "Then follow me, and keep close!"

The twins quickly pulled on their slippers and tiptoed after Tilly, careful not to make a sound. The little owl led them into the forest, which seemed to glow with a faint, magical light under the stars. The trees whispered softly as they passed, and the air was filled with the scent of pine and fresh dew.

They walked for a while, following Tilly's gentle hoots, until they reached the base of the enchanted mountains. There, nestled between two towering pines, was the entrance to the Cozy Cave of Dreams. A soft, golden glow seeped from the cave, casting a warm light over the mossy stones and the trees surrounding it. Luke and Lila's hearts swelled with wonder as they gazed at the cave's entrance, which seemed to invite them in with open arms.

"Welcome to the Cozy Cave," Tilly whispered, gesturing for them to follow her inside.

The moment they stepped into the cave, they felt a wave of warmth and calm wash over them. The walls were covered in soft, glowing moss that cast a gentle light, and crystals sparkled in shades of blue and purple, like little stars dotting the cave's interior. The floor was blanketed with soft, fluffy moss that felt as cozy as a warm blanket beneath their feet.

As they ventured deeper, they noticed the cave was filled with small nooks and hideaways, each one a cozy resting place. Some corners had hollow logs filled with plush leaves, others held piles of smooth, rounded stones that hummed a quiet lullaby. There were even warm nests woven from shimmering vines and sprinkled with feathers and petals.

"Welcome, Luke and Lila!" came a deep, gentle voice.

They looked up to see a large, gentle bear with soft, golden-brown fur and a friendly face. He wore a tiny pair of spectacles perched on his nose and a little vest that seemed to have pockets filled with lavender and sprigs of chamomile.

"I'm Bongo, the keeper of the Cozy Cave," he said with a warm smile. "I take care of this place and make sure everyone finds a cozy spot to rest."

Luke and Lila felt an instant warmth toward Bongo. His voice was soothing, like a melody of calm, and he looked at them with eyes full of kindness.

"Come," Bongo said, gesturing with his large paw. "Let me show you around."

He led them deeper into the cave, where they saw other animals already snuggled into cozy spots, each one looking as if they were wrapped in the comfort of a dream. There was a fox curled up in a nest of leaves, a family of rabbits nestled under a soft blanket of moss, and a raccoon snoozing in a hollow log filled with warm feathers.

Bongo showed them a little alcove with a bed made of smooth, round stones that hummed a gentle lullaby. "This is the Stone Song Bed," he explained. "Each stone has been smoothed by the river and placed here with care. They sing a lullaby to help anyone who rests here fall into a peaceful sleep."

Lila reached out to touch one of the stones, feeling the warmth of it against her hand. The humming tune was so soft and calming that she felt a gentle drowsiness settling over her.

Next, Bongo showed them a hollow log lined with layers of soft, plush leaves that looked as cozy as a nest. "This is the Leafy Log," he said, his voice filled with pride. "It's perfect for those who like a snug, quiet space. The leaves are from the oldest trees in the forest and carry the scent of earth and pine."

Luke leaned close, inhaling the soft, earthy scent of the leaves. It reminded him of autumn days and cozy nights by a campfire, and he felt a warmth spread through his chest.

"Would you like to try the Nest of Feathers?" Bongo asked, leading them to a small nook filled with a nest woven from vines and sprinkled with delicate feathers and flower petals. It looked as soft as a cloud, and the vines shimmered with a gentle glow.

"This nest is woven with special vines that hold the light of the stars," Bongo explained. "Those who sleep here often dream of gentle, starlit skies."

Luke and Lila looked at each other, eyes wide with excitement. They had never seen such magical places to rest, and each bed seemed to carry a different kind of comfort.

"You're welcome to choose whichever bed you like

best," Bongo said, his voice warm and encouraging. "Tonight, this cave is here just for you."

Luke chose the Leafy Log, curling up inside its snug walls, feeling the soft leaves cushion him like a warm embrace. He nestled his head down, inhaling the comforting scent of the forest, his body relaxing instantly.

Lila, on the other hand, couldn't resist the Nest of Feathers. She climbed in and felt the delicate feathers wrap around her, as soft as a whisper. She gazed up at the glowing vines, which sparkled like a sky full of stars, and felt herself drifting off, as if she were floating among the constellations.

Tilly, the little owl, perched on a nearby ledge, her voice as soft as a lullaby. "I'll sing you a song to help you drift into sleep," she said with a kind smile.

As Tilly began to sing, her voice filled the cave with a gentle melody. The song was soft and slow, like the whisper of the wind through the trees, and it carried with it a warmth that wrapped around Luke and Lila like a blanket. They listened to her soothing tune, their eyelids growing heavier with each note.

Bongo placed a soft paw on each of their heads, his touch comforting and gentle. "Rest well, little ones. The Cozy Cave will keep you safe and warm, and when you wake, you'll feel as if you've been wrapped in a dream."

As Tilly's song filled the air, Luke and Lila felt a peaceful drowsiness settling over them. Their eyes closed, and they felt as though they were sinking into the softest, coziest embrace, surrounded by warmth and light.

In their dreams, they floated through forests filled with shimmering stars, gentle animals guiding them along paths lined with soft moss and twinkling lights. They felt as though they were drifting through a world of peace and calm, each step filling them with warmth and happiness.

When they finally opened their eyes, they were back in their beds, the first light of dawn peeking through their window. They felt refreshed, their hearts full of memories of the Cozy Cave, Bongo the gentle bear, and Tilly's lullaby.

And from that night on, whenever they needed a little extra comfort, they would close their eyes and imagine the Cozy Cave of Dreams, filled with soft moss, glowing crystals, and the gentle warmth of their new friends. And soon, they'd drift into peaceful sleep, dreaming of magical caves, soft beds, and a world filled with warmth and light.

# The Magical Midnight Moth Parade

Rowan and his little sister, Emma, had always been curious children. They loved to climb trees, explore the woods, and make up stories about the stars. Every night, they'd sit by their bedroom window, looking out at the darkened meadow behind their house, imagining all the magical creatures that might live there. But one night, something truly magical happened—something that only came once every hundred years.

It was a quiet, calm night. The moon hung high in the sky, casting a gentle glow over the landscape, and a cool breeze whispered through the trees. As the clock in their room ticked closer to midnight, Rowan and Emma felt a tingle of excitement they couldn't explain. They were just about to crawl into bed when they heard a soft, fluttering knock at their window.

The children exchanged curious glances, their eyes wide with wonder. They tiptoed to the window and opened it carefully, letting the cool night air drift inside. To their amazement, a shimmering moth floated just outside, its wings glowing with a soft, silvery light. Its wings were covered in delicate patterns that looked like stars and constellations, and a trail of sparkling dust floated in its wake.

"Rowan, Emma," the moth whispered in a voice as soft as a lullaby, "would you like to come with me to the Midnight Moth Parade?"

Rowan and Emma's eyes sparkled with excitement. They had never heard of a Midnight Moth Parade, but it sounded magical, like something from one of their bedtime stories.

"Yes, please!" they replied eagerly.

The shimmering moth nodded, its wings flapping gently. "Then follow me," it said, floating back from the window and leading them outside.

Rowan and Emma quickly pulled on their slippers and jackets, then followed the moth across their yard and into the moonlit meadow. The path ahead was lined with flowers that seemed to glow under the silver light, their petals shimmering softly as if painted with stardust. The children walked hand in hand, their hearts racing with excitement and wonder as they followed the magical moth.

The path wound through tall grasses and trees, all bathed in a gentle, dreamy light. Along the way, they saw other moths drifting through the air, each one glowing softly, their wings decorated with tiny star-like patterns. Some were small and delicate, while others were large with wide, silken wings that seemed to ripple like waves in the wind. The air around them was filled with a soft, comforting hum, like the sound of a lullaby.

Finally, the shimmering moth stopped at the edge of a secret meadow. Rowan and Emma gasped in awe at the sight before them: the entire meadow was filled with moths, each one glowing in shades of silver, blue, and lavender, their wings twinkling with patterns that looked like tiny constellations. Thousands of moths floated gently in the air, filling the meadow with a soft, magical light.

"This is the Midnight Moth Parade," the moth whispered, its voice barely more than a soft breath. "Tonight, we gather to celebrate dreams and bring peaceful rest to the world."

Rowan and Emma felt a sense of calm wash over them as they gazed at the beautiful scene. The moths began to move in a gentle, graceful rhythm, their wings flapping in time with each other. It was like watching a dance, each moth's movements in perfect harmony with the next. As they flapped their wings, they released a fine, sparkling dust into the air, which drifted down like glittering snowflakes, casting a warm glow over the meadow.

"This dust is called dream dust," the shimmering moth explained. "It carries peaceful dreams and gentle wishes, spreading calm and comfort wherever it lands."

The moth handed each of the children a tiny glass jar, its lid topped with a delicate silver ribbon. "Here," it said, "you may collect some dream dust for yourselves. When you sprinkle it on your pillows tonight, it will bring sweet dreams and restful sleep."

Rowan and Emma took the jars carefully, feeling the smooth glass warm in their hands. They held them out, catching the dream dust as it floated down like tiny stars. The dust sparkled brightly, filling their jars with a soft glow, and each speck seemed to hum with a quiet, calming energy.

The moths continued their parade, forming gentle patterns in the air that looked like swirls of stardust and rings of glowing light. The air was filled with the soft sound of wings, a gentle, comforting hum that made Rowan and Emma feel as though they were floating on a cloud.

They watched as the moths formed constellations in the air, their wings tracing the shapes of familiar stars—Orion, the Big Dipper, and even a shooting star that seemed to streak across the meadow in a burst of silver light. It was like watching the night sky come alive, and the children felt as if they were standing in a world made entirely of dreams.

As the parade continued, Rowan and Emma began to feel a warm drowsiness settling over them. Their eyelids grew heavier with each gentle beat of the moths' wings, and they felt wrapped in a soft, cozy calm, as if they were being cradled by the night itself.

Sensing their sleepiness, the shimmering moth fluttered closer, its gentle voice a soft murmur. "The parade will soon end, and it will be time for you to return home," it said. "But remember, the dream dust you've collected will always bring you peace and sweet dreams whenever you need it."

Rowan and Emma nodded, their hearts full of gratitude and warmth. They held their jars close, feeling the gentle hum of the dream dust inside, like a lullaby captured in glass.

As the last of the moths flapped their wings in a slow, graceful circle, the shimmering moth guided Rowan and Emma back through the meadow and along the glowing path of flowers. The flowers seemed to bow as they passed, their petals sparkling with star-dust, as if saying goodbye.

When they reached the edge of their yard, the shimmering moth hovered just above them, its silvery wings casting a gentle light over the children.

"Thank you, Rowan and Emma, for joining the Midnight Moth Parade," it said with a kind smile. "Remember, you can always look to the stars for comfort, and let their light guide you."

The children nodded, their eyes growing heavy, but their hearts full of the magic they had just experienced. With a final flutter of its wings, the moth drifted back into the night, leaving a trail of sparkling dust that shimmered in the air.

Rowan and Emma climbed back into their beds, holding their jars of dream dust close. Carefully, they sprinkled a little on their pillows, watching as the dust sparkled and settled, casting a gentle glow over their blankets.

As they lay back, the soft, calming energy of the dream dust wrapped around them, like a warm hug from the night sky. They closed their eyes, feeling as if they were still in the magical meadow, surrounded by shimmering moths and gentle wings.

That night, they dreamed of the Midnight Moth Parade, of twinkling constellations, and of a world filled with soft, comforting light. And every time they looked at their jars of dream dust, they remembered the magical night they spent in the meadow, where the moths danced and the stars came alive.

From that night on, Rowan and Emma knew that no matter where they were, the magic of the Midnight Moth Parade would always be with them, bringing peace and sweet dreams whenever they needed it.

# The Secret Workshop of the Star Carvers

Every night, Maya and her little brother Kyle would gaze up at the stars from their bedroom window. They loved watching the sky as it filled with tiny, twinkling lights. Sometimes, they would pretend that the stars were the lights of distant ships sailing across a cosmic sea. Other times, they'd make up stories about where the stars came from and what kind of magic made them glow so brightly.

One chilly autumn evening, as they lay side by side in bed, Maya sighed. "I wish we could visit the place where stars are born. I bet it's magical."

Kyle's eyes sparkled with excitement at the thought. "Maybe there's a secret workshop, where someone makes each star one by one!"

They shared a dreamy smile before snuggling

under their blankets, thinking about all the different ways stars might come to life. As they drifted off, a soft light appeared in the room—a tiny glow that seemed to hover in the air. Neither of them noticed, too deep in their dreams, to realize something magical was happening.

In the morning, as they stirred awake, they each found a tiny star-shaped key resting under their pillows, glowing faintly. The keys were small, just the right size to fit in their palms, and felt warm to the touch.

"Maya! Look at this!" Kyle whispered, holding up his glowing key. Maya gasped and held up hers, too, her eyes wide with wonder.

Before they could even ask where the keys had come from, a gentle, warm light filled the room, guiding them toward the window. Together, holding their keys tightly, they followed the light out of their room and down a winding path that seemed to appear out of nowhere, leading toward the tallest mountain in the distance. The air was crisp and fresh, and the stars still glimmered faintly above, as if cheering them on.

After a journey that felt both long and short, they reached the base of the mountain, where an ancient stone staircase rose high into the misty clouds above. They took a deep breath and began to climb, their star keys lighting the way. The higher they went, the quieter the world became, until the only sound was the soft crunch of their footsteps and the occasional whisper of wind through the rocks.

Finally, as they reached the summit, they saw it—a grand wooden door set into the side of the mountain, carved with swirling patterns that looked like constellations. The door had a single keyhole in the shape of a star, glowing faintly, just like their keys.

Maya and Kyle exchanged excited smiles and inserted their keys into the door. As they turned them, the door creaked open, revealing the most magical sight they had ever seen.

Inside was a vast workshop filled with twinkling star fragments, glowing tools, and shimmering shelves lined with tiny, freshly carved stars. It was as if they had stepped into a sparkling galaxy, with every corner of the workshop illuminated by a soft, otherworldly glow. The air was filled with a gentle hum, like the sound of starlight itself.

"Welcome, welcome!" came a warm, cheerful voice from across the room.

Maya and Kyle turned to see an owl with feathers as silver as moonlight, perched on a workbench. He wore a tiny pair of glasses balanced on his beak and a small apron covered in silver dust. Beside him stood a fox with a bushy, sparkling tail and a squirrel with a tiny hammer tucked into its belt.

"We're the Star Carvers," the owl explained with a gentle smile. "I'm Orin, and these are my fellow artisans, Fern and Trixie."

The fox, Fern, gave a friendly nod, and Trixie, the squirrel, waved excitedly with her tiny hammer. "Welcome to our workshop!" she squeaked. "We make every star you see in the sky, each one carved and polished by hand."

Maya and Kyle's eyes grew wide with wonder as they looked around, their hearts racing with excitement. All around them, shelves sparkled with tiny stars in various stages of creation—some were rough and unpolished, others gleamed with a finished glow. On a nearby table, a pile of star fragments shimmered like piles of glittering snow.

"Would you like to help us make some stars?" Fern asked, her golden eyes warm and inviting.

"Yes, please!" Maya and Kyle replied eagerly.

Orin guided them to a workbench, where the tools lay waiting. Each tool was made from stardust and crystals, with handles that glowed in shades of blue, purple, and silver. Orin handed Maya a small, delicate brush and Kyle a tiny chisel, both glowing softly in their hands.

"Every star holds a tiny dream," Orin explained. "Some are dreams of joy, others of adventure or peace. We carve the stars, polish them, and then fill them with these dreams so they can shine down on the world."

Maya and Kyle's eyes sparkled as they listened. They each picked up a small, rough star fragment from the pile and began to work, carefully carving and shaping it. As they worked, Trixie scurried over with a jar of "star polish," which looked like liquid starlight, shimmering and swirling in shades of silver and gold.

"Once you're done carving, you can polish it with this," Trixie explained, dipping a tiny cloth into the polish and dabbing it onto one of the stars. The moment the polish touched the star, it began to glow, casting a warm, comforting light that seemed to fill the room.

Maya and Kyle carefully polished their stars, watching as they transformed from rough fragments into beautiful, glowing gems. Each star seemed to pulse with a soft light, as if it had come to life in their hands.

As they continued working, Orin handed them a tiny pouch filled with "wish dust." "This is what gives each star its magic," he explained. "It's made from the wishes and dreams of children all around the world.

Sprinkle a little onto your star, and think of a wish you'd like to send with it."

Maya closed her eyes, holding her star close. She thought of joy and laughter, of happy days spent exploring with Kyle. She sprinkled a pinch of wish dust over her star, and it glowed a little brighter, casting a warm light that made her feel cozy and safe.

Kyle held his star in both hands, thinking of adventure and kindness, of exploring new places and meeting new friends. He sprinkled his wish dust over the star, watching as it shimmered with a spark of excitement, like a little beacon of hope.

When they were finished, Fern led them to the balcony of the workshop, where the night sky stretched out before them, filled with countless stars. The mountains below were cloaked in a soft mist, and the world felt calm and peaceful under the watchful glow of the stars.

"Now, it's time to send your stars into the sky," Fern said gently, her voice filled with pride. "They'll find their way to the perfect place, where they'll shine down on someone who needs them."

Maya and Kyle held their stars out, feeling a mixture of excitement and wonder. They each took a deep breath, then let go, watching as their stars floated up, joining the others in the night sky. The stars drifted higher and higher, glowing brighter with each second, until they were just tiny twinkles in the distance, blending in with the vast constellations above.

As they watched their stars take their places in the sky, Orin placed a gentle wing on each of their shoulders. "Thank you for helping us tonight," he said warmly. "You've created stars filled with kindness and joy, and those are the brightest stars of all."

Maya and Kyle felt a wave of pride and happiness, knowing that they had made something special, something that would bring light and dreams to others.

The gentle hum of the workshop began to lull them into a peaceful drowsiness, their eyes growing heavier as the calm of the mountain wrapped around them. Fern and Trixie guided them back to the entrance of the workshop, where their star-shaped keys glowed softly in the starlight.

"Whenever you look up at the stars, remember that you helped create some of that light," Trixie said with a smile. "And you're always welcome here in the workshop of the Star Carvers."

Maya and Kyle nodded sleepily, their hearts full of warmth and joy. They waved goodbye to their new friends, and with one last look at the glowing workshop, they began their journey back down the mountain, the soft light of their star keys guiding them.

The world was quiet and still, wrapped in the gentle glow of the stars they had helped create. By the time they reached home, they could barely keep their eyes open. They slipped back into bed, holding their star keys close, feeling the warmth of the workshop still lingering in their hearts.

That night, they dreamed of the secret workshop high in the mountains, of glittering star fragments and tiny jars of wish dust, of friends who carved and polished the stars, filling the sky with light and hope.

And from that night on, whenever Maya and Kyle looked up at the stars, they felt a special kind of magic, knowing that some of that light came from the stars they had created together.

# The Moonlit Forest Circus

Luca and Zoe were twins who shared a love for adventure. They had always been curious and playful, constantly exploring the world around them. Their backyard, with its tall trees and wild bushes, was their favorite place to play. They would imagine it was a jungle, a pirate island, or a castle—whatever their hearts desired. But nothing excited them more than going to the circus. They loved the flashing lights, the lively music, and the talented performers who could do things they never thought possible.

One warm summer night, Luca and Zoe convinced their parents to let them camp in their backyard. They set up a cozy tent under the big oak tree and filled it with blankets and pillows. With their lanterns flickering beside them and the stars twinkling above, they felt as if they were in their own little world. They whispered stories and giggled under the covers until, slowly, their voices faded, and they began to drift into sleep.

Just as their eyes were about to close, a soft, silvery glow appeared between the trees, lighting up the darkness. Luca was the first to notice it. "Zoe, look!" he whispered, nudging his sister awake.

Zoe rubbed her eyes and peeked out of the tent. "What's that light?" she asked, her voice filled with wonder.

Without a word, they climbed out of the tent and tiptoed toward the glowing light, their hearts racing with excitement. The light seemed to dance between the trees, leading them deeper into the woods. They followed, their steps quiet, as if they were afraid the magic might disappear if they made too much noise.

Finally, they emerged into a clearing and gasped in amazement. There, under the bright, full moon, was the most magical sight they had ever seen—the Moonlit Forest Circus.

The clearing was alive with lights and colors, as fireflies twinkled like fairy lights strung between the trees. The air was filled with the gentle hum of music, played by animals they had only ever seen in books. A large banner hung between two tall trees, painted with letters that seemed to shimmer under the moonlight: *Welcome to the Moonlit Forest Circus.*

"Welcome, Luca and Zoe," came a warm, deep voice from the center of the clearing.

They turned to see a wise old fox standing on his hind legs, dressed in a tiny top hat and a dapper red vest. He carried a small cane, and his eyes sparkled with kindness and wisdom.

"I am Rollo, the ringmaster of the Moonlit Forest Circus," he said with a bow. "Tonight, you are our honorary guests. The Moonlit Forest Circus only appears under a full moon, and we are delighted to share our magic with you."

Luca and Zoe beamed with excitement. They couldn't believe their luck—stumbling upon a secret circus run by animals! It was like a dream come true.

Rollo led them to a pair of cozy seats made from soft moss and leaves, set perfectly for viewing the magical show. "Please, make yourselves comfortable. Tonight's performance is dedicated to you."

As they settled in, the gentle hum of music grew louder, and from the shadows, a group of squirrels leaped into the clearing, their fluffy tails twitching with energy. They were acrobats, bouncing gracefully from one tree branch to another, swinging on vines, and flipping through the air in perfect harmony. Each time they landed, the fireflies swirled around them, creating sparkling trails of light that made their movements look like shooting stars.

The twins watched in awe as the squirrels performed their routine, twirling and somersaulting in the moonlight. Zoe clapped her hands in delight, her eyes shining with wonder. "They're amazing!" she whispered to Luca, who was just as mesmerized.

Next, a family of bears lumbered into the clearing, balancing pinecones on their noses and juggling them with ease. The smallest bear, who wore a bow around her neck, balanced on a fallen log while tossing pinecones in the air, catching each one with a big, proud smile. The other bears clapped along, creating a gentle, rhythmic beat that made the pinecones dance in the air.

"Bravo, bravo!" Luca and Zoe cheered, their laughter filling the clearing.

After the bears, a group of rabbits hopped in, carrying tiny bouquets of flowers and leaves. With a wave of his cane, Rollo announced, "And now, for the incredible magical talents of the Moonlit Magicians!"

The rabbits gathered in a circle, their little paws moving in unison as they twisted the flowers and leaves, making them bloom into larger, more colorful arrangements. With a gentle flick of their ears, they tossed the flowers into the air, where they burst into delicate petals that floated down like confetti. It was as if they had turned the clearing into a garden of magical blooms.

One of the rabbits hopped over to Zoe, handing her a tiny flower crown made of glowing blue flowers. "For you, Miss Zoe," he said with a shy smile.

Zoe put on the crown, feeling like a queen. "Thank you," she whispered, enchanted by the magic of it all.

After the rabbits' dazzling display, Rollo turned to Luca and Zoe with a twinkle in his eye. "And now, dear guests, it's time for you to join in the fun!"

Luca and Zoe exchanged excited looks, thrilled at the idea of being part of the Moonlit Forest Circus.

Rollo handed Luca a small drum, its surface decorated with tiny stars that glowed in the dark. "Luca, you shall be our drummer for the night, leading the marching band."

Then he turned to Zoe and gave her a shiny tambourine, its edge lined with tiny bells that jingled softly. "And Zoe, you'll be joining our acrobats, adding a bit of sparkle to their show."

With Rollo leading the way, Luca tapped a steady beat on his drum, filling the clearing with a gentle, rhythmic sound. The fireflies began to swirl around him, forming a glowing path for the animals to follow.

One by one, the animals joined in, forming a grand parade that moved in time with Luca's beat.

The squirrels swung through the trees, twirling in mid-air, while the rabbits danced along the ground, their little feet tapping in perfect harmony. The bears clapped their paws, keeping time with the beat, and the entire clearing filled with the sounds of music, laughter, and joy.

Zoe shook her tambourine, adding a bright, cheerful jingle to the parade. As she moved with the acrobats, the fireflies danced around her, creating tiny bursts of light with each shake of the tambourine. She felt as if she were part of the magic, her laughter blending with the music as they paraded around the clearing.

As the parade continued, Luca and Zoe felt a warm, sleepy glow fill their hearts. The gentle rhythm of the drum, the soft jingle of the tambourine, and the soothing hum of the fireflies created a lullaby that seemed to wrap around them like a cozy blanket.

The parade came to a gentle end as the animals gathered in a circle around the twins. Rollo stepped forward, bowing with a warm smile. "Thank you, Luca and Zoe, for joining us tonight. Your laughter and joy have made this night truly magical."

The twins beamed with happiness, their eyelids

growing heavy as the warmth of the Moonlit Forest Circus wrapped around them.

Rollo guided them to a soft, mossy bed near the edge of the clearing. "Rest here for a while, my friends," he said softly. "The magic of the forest will watch over you."

Luca and Zoe lay down on the moss, feeling its softness beneath them, like the fluffiest blanket. The fireflies gathered above, their lights dimming to a gentle glow, casting a peaceful light over the clearing. The animals settled around them, forming a cozy, protective circle.

Rollo began to hum a soft lullaby, his voice blending with the sounds of the forest—the rustle of leaves, the whisper of the breeze, and the quiet hum of the fireflies. The gentle music lulled Luca and Zoe into a deep, peaceful drowsiness, their eyes closing as they drifted into sleep.

As the moon dipped lower in the sky, the forest grew quieter, wrapped in the warmth and magic of the Moonlit Forest Circus. When the first light of dawn appeared on the horizon, Rollo gently nudged the twins awake, his kind eyes sparkling in the early morning glow.

"It's time to return home," he whispered softly.

"But remember, you'll always be honorary guests of the Moonlit Forest Circus."

Luca and Zoe rubbed their eyes, feeling as if they had woken from the best dream. They said goodbye to Rollo and the animals, giving each of them a hug. With one last smile, Rollo led them back to the path, where the fireflies guided them toward home.

When they reached their tent, they found themselves back in their cozy sleeping bags, the first rays of sunlight streaming through the trees. They closed their eyes, feeling the warmth of the moss, the jingling of the tambourine, and the steady beat of the drum still in their hearts.

That morning, they woke with smiles on their faces, their minds filled with memories of the Moonlit Forest Circus. And from that day on, whenever they saw fireflies dancing in the evening or heard the gentle sounds of the forest, they'd remember the magical night they spent with their friends under the full moon.

And as they drifted off to sleep each night, they'd dream of acrobatic squirrels, juggling bears, and a wise old fox who invited them to the most enchanting circus in the world.

# The Dream-Collecting Firebird

In a small, quiet village nestled between gentle hills and shady forests, there was a legend told to children at bedtime—a legend of the Dream-Collecting Firebird. They said it was a magical creature with feathers that glowed in beautiful shades of orange, pink, and gold, like a sunset woven into wings. It was said that the Firebird visited children with kind hearts to collect their dreams, so it could share peace and joy across the world.

Ten-year-old Callie and her best friend Sam had grown up hearing the stories. They loved the idea of a magical Firebird, flying through the sky to spread dreams and happiness. They'd even imagined seeing it one day, gliding above their village, leaving trails of light behind it.

One cool autumn evening, as the village grew quiet and the stars began to blink in the night sky, Callie and Sam were in Callie's room, whispering and laughing about their day. Suddenly, they heard a soft, gentle chirping sound just outside the window. Startled, they both turned to see the source of the noise—and gasped in amazement.

There, perched on the windowsill, was the Dream-Collecting Firebird. It was even more beautiful than they had imagined. Its feathers shimmered with a warm glow, flickering with shades of orange, pink, and gold that seemed to pulse like a gentle flame. The Firebird's eyes sparkled with kindness, and it radiated a soft warmth that filled the room with a comforting glow.

Callie and Sam held their breath, too awestruck to speak. The Firebird tilted its head, looking at them with gentle eyes, and then gave a soft chirp as if inviting them closer.

With a mixture of excitement and wonder, Callie approached the Firebird. "Are... are you the Dream-Collecting Firebird?" she whispered.

The Firebird nodded, its eyes twinkling with warmth, and then it extended one of its wings, inviting them to come closer. Callie and Sam exchanged a quick, excited look, then reached out to touch the beautiful feathers. They were soft and warm, and seemed to hum with a gentle, magical energy.

The Firebird chirped again, then lowered its body, making room on its back for them to climb on. Callie and Sam hesitated for only a moment before carefully climbing onto its back, settling into the soft feathers. They felt safe and cozy, as if the Firebird was cradling them in a gentle embrace.

With a powerful beat of its wings, the Firebird rose into the air, carrying them out of the window and into the night sky. The village grew smaller below them as they soared higher, the rooftops and treetops blending into a patchwork of dark green and silver under the moonlight. The air was crisp and filled with the scent of autumn leaves, and as they flew, Callie and Sam felt as though they were floating through a dream.

The stars above sparkled like tiny lanterns, guiding them as they glided through the sky. The Firebird's feathers glowed softly, casting a warm light around them that made the night feel as cozy as a blanket. Callie held onto the feathers in front of her, feeling the gentle rise and fall of the Firebird's wings, while Sam leaned back, looking up at the stars with wide, joyful eyes.

As they flew over a sleeping town nestled in a valley, the Firebird slowed, chirping softly. Callie and

Sam looked down and gasped—they could see tiny, glowing orbs floating up from the houses below. Each orb was a different color, casting a soft light as it drifted up into the night.

"What are those?" Sam asked in awe, reaching out toward the glowing orbs.

The Firebird chirped in response, and in that moment, Callie understood. "They're dreams!" she whispered excitedly. "The dreams of everyone sleeping in the town!"

The Firebird nodded, its eyes filled with warmth. It tilted its head, guiding them to look at a small, golden satchel that hung around its neck. The satchel sparkled and hummed, as if it were alive with magic.

"We're helping the Firebird collect the dreams!" Callie realized, her heart swelling with joy.

With a gentle wave of its wing, the Firebird guided the glowing dreams toward the satchel. Callie and Sam watched as each dream floated down, entering the satchel and adding its own soft light to the glow. The satchel seemed to hum with a happy energy, each dream adding its warmth and kindness to the collection.

The Firebird continued its journey, flying over forests and fields, with Callie and Sam helping to gather dreams along the way. As they flew over a peaceful village surrounded by tall, dark pine trees, Sam noticed a particularly bright dream—a radiant blue orb that shimmered with a calming light.

"That one must be a dream of happiness," he whispered, watching as it floated gently into the Firebird's satchel.

Callie pointed to a soft pink dream, glowing with a warm, gentle light. "And that one... maybe it's a dream of love," she guessed, smiling as it joined the others.

The Firebird chirped softly, as if confirming their thoughts, and continued to glide over the quiet countryside, collecting dreams from every sleeping home they passed. Callie and Sam felt a deep sense of peace, knowing that each dream they collected would be shared with those who needed it most, spreading happiness, kindness, and calm across the world.

As they flew, the Firebird began to tell them about its mission, using soft chirps and gentle gestures to convey its message. It explained that each dream held a tiny wish, a spark of hope or joy. By gathering these dreams and spreading them across the world, the Firebird helped to create a sense of warmth and connection, so that everyone—no matter where they were—could feel the magic of kindness and happiness.

Callie and Sam listened intently, their hearts filled with awe. They understood now why the Dream-

Collecting Firebird was so important, and they felt honored to be part of its journey.

As the night wore on, they began to feel a gentle drowsiness settle over them, a cozy warmth that made them want to snuggle into the Firebird's feathers and close their eyes. But before they could drift off, the Firebird slowed, bringing them to the top of a hill bathed in moonlight.

They landed softly, and the Firebird gently lowered them to the ground. With a final, warm chirp, it reached into its satchel and pulled out two small feathers, each one glowing with a soft, golden light.

"These are for you," the Firebird seemed to say, offering the feathers to Callie and Sam. The feathers were warm in their hands, radiating a gentle, calming energy that made them feel as if they were still soaring through the night sky.

"Thank you, Firebird," Callie whispered, holding her feather close. Sam nodded, his eyes shining with gratitude. "We'll never forget this night."

The Firebird gave a soft chirp, its eyes filled with kindness, and then, with a graceful sweep of its wings, it rose back into the sky. Callie and Sam watched as it glided into the distance, its glowing feathers leaving a trail of light behind, like the final brushstrokes of a sunset.

Feeling a gentle pull, they walked back down the hill, holding their glowing feathers tightly in their hands. They found themselves back in Callie's room, snuggled in their blankets, their hearts still warm with the memory of the Firebird and their magical journey.

As they drifted into sleep, they dreamed of glowing skies, gentle wings, and a golden satchel filled with dreams of kindness, peace, and joy. And from that night on, whenever they looked up at the stars, they felt a special warmth, knowing that somewhere, the Dream-Collecting Firebird was flying through the night, gathering dreams to share with the world.

And as they held their glowing feathers close, they knew they'd carry the magic of that night with them always, spreading their own kindness and joy wherever they went.

# The Whispering Wind of Wonder

Lucky loved listening to the wind. Every night, as he lay in bed, he would hear the gentle breeze singing through his bedroom window, rustling the leaves outside and making soft, soothing sounds that lulled him to sleep. It felt like the wind was telling him stories, carrying secrets and dreams from faraway places.

But one evening, the wind sounded different. As he lay under his cozy blanket, he heard a soft whisper—almost like his name, carried on a gentle breeze. *Lucky... Lucky...*

Curious, he sat up and looked out his window. The wind seemed to be swirling in a special way, twisting and curling through the trees, as if waiting for him. With a quiet sense of wonder, Lucky tiptoed out of bed, slipped into his slippers, and opened the door to step outside.

The moment he did, the wind wrapped around him, gentle and cool, like a soft hug. It felt as if the breeze was alive, full of magic, and it made him feel safe and excited all at once.

"Hello, Lucky," the wind whispered, its voice soft and kind. "I am the Whispering Wind of Wonder, and tonight, I would like to show you a place where dreams are born and wishes come true."

Lucky's heart filled with excitement, and he could barely believe his ears. "Really? You want to take me there?"

The Whispering Wind rustled around him, lifting him gently off the ground. "Yes, Lucky. Tonight, you will be my guest."

With a gentle whoosh, the wind swept him up into the night sky. Lucky felt weightless, as if he were floating on a cloud. The stars above sparkled brightly, and the moon cast a soft, silvery glow over the world below. The wind carried him higher, and soon he was gliding through the sky, wrapped in the comforting embrace of the magical breeze.

As they soared higher, Lucky looked around in awe. Fluffy clouds drifted by, each one shaped like a different animal—there was a lion, a rabbit, even an elephant with big, soft ears that looked as if they were waving hello. He smiled as they floated past, feeling as if he had stepped into a magical dreamland.

After a while, the Whispering Wind took him through a series of rainbows that shimmered and sparkled in the moonlight. The colors glowed with a soft, magical light, casting a warm, comforting glow over everything. Lucky reached out to touch the rainbows, feeling their warmth and watching as they left little trails of color on his fingers.

The Whispering Wind whispered softly in his ear, "Tonight, I'm taking you to the Valley of Wishes, a special place where wishes are gathered and shared with the world."

They floated gently down toward a hidden valley below, where the ground sparkled with a gentle, glowing light. The valley was filled with soft, rolling hills covered in grass that shimmered in shades of blue and silver under the moonlight. The air was filled with a quiet hum, like the gentle murmur of a thousand whispered wishes.

The Whispering Wind carried him to the center of the valley, where dozens of glowing, glass jars were scattered, each one shimmering with a unique color. As Lucky watched, tiny gusts of wind drifted down from the sky, each one carrying a whisper—a wish from someone in the world below.

The wishes floated gently toward the jars, and Lucky could see each one glow softly as it settled inside, filling the jar with a warm, comforting light. Each jar seemed to hold its own unique glow, like tiny, colorful stars resting in glass.

"Would you like to help me collect the wishes?" the Whispering Wind asked, its voice filled with kindness.

Lucky nodded eagerly. "Yes, please!"

The Whispering Wind showed him how to reach out and catch each wish, gently guiding it into a glass jar. The wishes came in many forms: tiny whispers, soft sighs, even little bursts of light. Each one felt warm in his hands, like holding a tiny spark of hope or happiness.

As he worked, Lucky noticed that each jar glowed with a different color. One jar was filled with a warm, golden light that made him feel safe and happy. Another jar glowed with a soft, peaceful blue, like the calm of a quiet lake. There were jars filled with gentle shades of pink, green, and purple, each one casting its own soothing glow.

"What are these wishes for?" Lucky asked as he placed a wish into a jar that glowed with a cheerful yellow light.

The Whispering Wind's voice was soft and warm as it explained. "Each wish carries a special hope or dream. Some are wishes for bravery, some are for happiness, and others are wishes for love and kindness. Every wish is sent from the heart, and my job is to gather them, so they can be shared with those who need them most."

Lucky felt a warm glow in his chest as he listened, his heart filling with a sense of peace. He understood now that each wish was a gift, a little spark of hope that could brighten someone's life.

He continued to catch wishes, guiding them gently into their jars, feeling a different kind of warmth with each one. There was a wish for laughter, which filled him with a happy energy, making him want to giggle. Another wish was for calm, which felt like the soft touch of a comforting hug. He even found a wish for adventure, which sparked a little thrill of excitement in his heart.

As he worked, Lucky noticed one jar that glowed with an especially bright, radiant light. It was filled with wishes for love and kindness, and the jar shimmered with a beautiful, rosy pink glow. Holding it close, he felt a warmth that wrapped around him like a soft blanket, filling him with a deep sense of peace.

"These wishes will bring joy to those who receive

them," the Whispering Wind said gently. "Just as the stars light up the night sky, these wishes light up the hearts of those who need them."

Lucky continued to gather wishes, feeling his heart grow lighter with each one. The valley around him sparkled with a warm, comforting glow, and he felt as if he were surrounded by the kindness and happiness of a thousand dreams.

As he placed the last wish into its jar, Lucky felt a gentle drowsiness settling over him. His eyes grew heavy, and he stifled a yawn, feeling the comforting warmth of the valley wrapping around him like a cozy blanket.

The Whispering Wind noticed his sleepiness and gave a soft, comforting whisper. "It's time for you to return home, Lucky, but don't worry—the magic of the Valley of Wishes will stay with you."

With a gentle lift, the wind carried him back up into the sky, cradling him in its soft, cool embrace. The valley below faded into a dreamy glow, and soon they were floating among the clouds once more. The animal-shaped clouds drifted by, and the rainbow paths sparkled in the distance, their colors casting a soothing glow over the night.

As they glided back toward his house, the Whispering Wind wrapped around him, its voice a soft lullaby. "Thank you, Lucky, for helping me gather the wishes tonight. I'll leave a gentle breeze by your window, so you'll always feel the magic of the Valley of Wishes."

With those words, the Whispering Wind gently set him down on his bedroom floor, the cool, comforting breeze wrapping around him like a final, gentle hug. Lucky climbed back into bed, feeling the warmth of the wishes and the peace of the valley filling his heart.

As he lay there, he heard the soft murmur of the Whispering Wind outside his window, a reminder of the magical night he had just experienced. He closed his eyes, holding onto the warmth and kindness of the wishes he had gathered, feeling as if he were wrapped in the glow of a thousand dreams.

That night, Lucky's dreams were filled with colorful jars, glowing valleys, and gentle winds that carried wishes across the world. And from that night on, whenever he heard the wind whispering outside his window, he knew it was the Whispering Wind of Wonder, carrying dreams and spreading kindness, just as it had shown him.

And as he drifted off to sleep each night, he felt a gentle breeze by his window, a comforting reminder of the magic of wishes and the joy of sharing dreams.

# The Midnight Jellyfish Ball

Sarah had always been captivated by the ocean. She loved everything about it—the gentle waves, the way the moonlight shimmered on the surface, and the soft hum of the water as it lapped against the shore. She had a collection of seashells back home and had filled countless sketchbooks with drawings of sea creatures, coral reefs, and imagined underwater kingdoms.

One warm summer night, while on vacation with her family, Sarah couldn't sleep. The soft sound of waves called to her, so she tiptoed out of her room and made her way to the beach. The moon was high and full, casting a silvery glow over the sand, and the world felt calm, as if it were holding its breath.

As she wandered along the shore, Sarah noticed something glinting in the moonlight, half-buried in the sand. Curious, she picked it up. It was a small, delicate glass bottle, sealed with a glowing wax seal that shimmered like the stars. Inside, she could see a rolled-up piece of paper, glowing faintly. Her heart skipped with excitement as she opened the bottle and carefully pulled out the paper.

Unrolling it, she saw beautiful, looping handwriting that seemed to dance across the page. The message read:

*"You are invited to the Midnight Jellyfish Ball! Follow the light, and come dance with us under the sea."*

Sarah's eyes sparkled with excitement. A jellyfish ball? Could it be real? Just as she finished reading, a soft, gentle glow appeared in the water near her feet. She looked up, and there, bobbing in the shallow waves, was a shimmering jellyfish, its delicate body glowing with soft shades of blue and pink, like a living lantern.

The jellyfish drifted closer, as if inviting her to follow. Sarah took a deep breath, her heart racing with excitement, and stepped into the water. The jellyfish glided forward, and as it did, she felt a strange, magical sensation, as if the water were carrying her, lifting her with a gentle, buoyant embrace. She took another step, and then another, feeling lighter with each one, until she found herself drifting alongside the jellyfish, gliding effortlessly under the water.

To her amazement, she could breathe easily, as if the ocean itself were wrapping her in a bubble of air. The jellyfish led her deeper into the sea, its glow lighting the way. Around her, fish darted and danced, their scales catching the light as they shimmered in every color imaginable. Coral reefs rose up like castles, with branches stretching out in soft hues of lavender, pink, and green. Everything felt alive, glowing gently in the underwater moonlight, as if the whole ocean were part of the invitation.

"Where are we going?" Sarah whispered to the jellyfish, though she wasn't sure it could answer.

In response, the jellyfish pulsed with a brighter glow, as if to say, *We're almost there.* They floated past an underwater forest of kelp, swaying gently in the current like the trees in a magical forest. Tiny bubbles rose around them, drifting upward and catching the moonlight that filtered through the water.

Finally, they reached a vast, open space, and Sarah gasped in wonder. They had arrived at the Jellyfish Ballroom.

The ballroom was an enormous underwater hall, bordered by shimmering coral walls and carpeted with a bed of soft, glowing sand. Above them, jellyfish of every shape and size floated gracefully, their translucent bodies shimmering in shades of blue, purple, pink, and gold. Some were small, no larger than Sarah's hand, while others were as big as beach umbrellas, their long, trailing tentacles moving like ribbons in a gentle breeze.

The jellyfish created a beautiful, glowing tapestry in the water, their light mingling and swirling in delicate patterns that looked like the night sky. It was as if Sarah had stepped into a living painting, with colors and shapes that shifted and flowed in perfect harmony.

Her jellyfish friend drifted closer, twirling slowly as if inviting her to dance. Sarah watched, captivated, and then, feeling brave, she began to mimic its movements. She stretched out her arms and spun gently, letting the water carry her as she floated and twirled in time with the jellyfish.

As she danced, the other jellyfish gathered around her, moving in graceful, rhythmic patterns, their tentacles creating soft trails of light that drifted around her like sparkles in the water. Some of the jellyfish floated close, their light brushing over her hands and arms, filling her with a gentle, comforting warmth.

The jellyfish began to hum a soft melody, a gentle, soothing tune that filled the water like a lullaby. Sarah could feel the music in her heart, each note wrapping around her like a cozy blanket. The melody was calm and peaceful, and it made her feel as though she were part of something magical, something ancient and beautiful.

As she danced, she lost track of time, feeling only the gentle sway of the water and the warmth of the jellyfish around her. She drifted through the ballroom, twirling and gliding with her new friends, each movement filling her with a deeper sense of calm.

One of the larger jellyfish floated down beside her, its glow a soft, dreamy blue. It extended a few of its tentacles, gently wrapping them around her hand, and guided her in a graceful circle. Sarah giggled, feeling like she was in a dance with the stars themselves. She looked around and saw the other jellyfish forming rings of light, spinning and twirling together in patterns that seemed to tell a story.

Her jellyfish friend, the one who had led her to the ballroom, pulsed with a warm, golden light and drifted close, humming the soft melody along with the others. Sarah followed its lead, twirling in gentle circles, feeling the water swirl around her like a comforting embrace. The light from the jellyfish bathed her in warmth, and she felt a cozy drowsiness beginning to settle over her, like the calm that comes just before sleep.

As the ball continued, the colors of the jellyfish grew softer, their lights dimming to a gentle glow. The melody slowed, becoming even softer, like a lullaby meant just for her. Sarah felt her eyelids growing heavy, but she didn't want the dance to end. She wanted to stay in the Jellyfish Ballroom forever, wrapped in the peaceful glow and the gentle hum of her underwater friends.

Sensing her drowsiness, the jellyfish that had brought her to the ball drifted closer, wrapping a few of its soft tentacles around her hand, as if to say, *It's time to go home now.*

Sarah nodded sleepily, feeling a deep gratitude for the magical experience she had been given. The jellyfish led her out of the ballroom, guiding her back through the coral reefs and past the swaying kelp. As they floated upward, the water grew lighter, and Sarah saw the silvery moonlight shining through the surface, like a gentle reminder of home.

Finally, they reached the shore, and the jellyfish released her hand, giving one last, gentle glow as it drifted back into the ocean. Sarah stood on the sand, watching as her friend floated away, its golden light growing fainter until it was just a tiny glimmer in the distance.

"Thank you," she whispered, feeling a warm glow in her heart.

The beach was quiet, and the waves lapped softly at her feet as she made her way back to her blanket under the stars. She lay down, feeling the soft sand beneath her and the gentle sea breeze around her. As she closed her eyes, she could still feel the gentle sway of the water, the warm glow of the jellyfish, and the soft melody of their lullaby.

With a contented sigh, Sarah drifted into a deep, peaceful sleep, her dreams filled with glowing seas, swirling lights, and the beautiful dance of the Midnight Jellyfish Ball. And as she slept, she knew that whenever she looked at the ocean, she would remember this magical night and the friends she had made beneath the waves.

From that night on, Sarah kept a small shell by her bed, a reminder of the Jellyfish Ballroom and the wonderful creatures who had shared their dance with her. And every time she heard the ocean's lullaby, she felt a comforting warmth, like the gentle glow of a jellyfish guiding her into peaceful dreams.

# The Owl and the Starlight Library

Greg loved staring up at the stars. Every night, he'd sit by his bedroom window, gazing into the endless sky, imagining all the stories the stars held in their glow. To him, each tiny light looked like a page in a book, waiting to be read.

One evening, as he sat by his window, something unusual caught his eye. Perched on a branch of the tree outside was a large owl with soft, shimmering feathers and wise, twinkling eyes. The owl held a golden book in its talons, and as it blinked at Greg, he felt as if it were studying him, deciding something important.

Suddenly, the owl spread its wings and glided down to his window, landing silently on the sill. Greg's eyes widened as the owl gently set the golden book aside, leaned forward, and presented him with a beautiful feather that glistened in shades of silver and blue. Tied to the feather was a small, shining bookmark, and Greg could feel a gentle warmth radiating from it as he took it in his hands.

"Hello, Greg," the owl said in a voice that was as soft as a whisper and as comforting as a lullaby. "I am Orpheus, the Keeper of the Starlight Library. Tonight, you are invited to visit."

Greg's heart raced with excitement. "The Starlight Library?" he asked, hardly believing what he was hearing.

Orpheus nodded, his eyes twinkling. "Yes. It is a place hidden among the stars, where dreams are stored in books, each one waiting for someone like you. Would you like to come?"

Greg's eyes shone with wonder. "Yes, please!" he whispered.

With a graceful nod, Orpheus opened his wings and motioned for Greg to climb onto his back. Greg took a deep breath, and with his feather bookmark still clutched in his hand, he climbed onto the owl's broad, soft back, feeling the warmth of the feathers beneath him.

Orpheus spread his wings wide, and with a gentle leap, they were off, gliding upward into the sky. The world below grew smaller and smaller as they rose higher, passing through wispy clouds that felt as soft as cotton and cool as night air. Stars sparkled around them, close enough to touch, casting a gentle glow over everything. Greg felt as if he were floating in a dream, surrounded by twinkling lights that whispered secrets only he could hear.

As they soared higher, Greg noticed shapes in the stars—constellations forming patterns that seemed to tell stories of their own. He saw a bear, a lion, and even a wise old turtle, each one twinkling softly in the darkness.

Finally, they reached a place high above the clouds, where the stars seemed to gather more closely together, forming a soft, glowing mist. In the center of it all was a grand, floating library made entirely of starlight. It was a beautiful, shimmering structure, with tall shelves made of glowing silver threads, each one filled with books that glowed in colors Greg had never seen before.

"This is the Starlight Library," Orpheus said gently, landing at the entrance and letting Greg slide off his back. "Here, each book holds a dream, ready to guide your night's journey."

Greg stepped inside, his heart brimming with excitement. The air was filled with the soft, comforting scent of old books, mixed with a hint of stardust. The shelves stretched high above him, filled with books that glowed in every imaginable shade—some a soft, calming blue, others a warm, golden yellow, and even a few that shimmered in gentle shades of lavender and green.

As he wandered through the aisles, Greg noticed that each book seemed to hum with a quiet magic, as if waiting patiently for someone to open it. Each title was written in a delicate, looping script, describing the kind of dream it held inside: *A Walk Through the Enchanted Forest, The Sky Ship Adventure, The Garden of Light.*

Orpheus guided Greg to a cozy corner filled with soft pillows that shimmered like stars. "Take your time, Greg," he said. "Choose any book that calls to you. Its story will shape your dreams tonight."

Greg ran his fingers along the spines of the books, feeling a gentle warmth from each one. After a few moments, a particular book caught his eye—a beautiful, glowing blue book titled *The Moonlit Forest.* The cover was decorated with a silver tree, its branches spreading out in delicate patterns, with tiny stars scattered among its leaves.

"This one," Greg said, holding the book close. It felt warm and inviting in his hands, as if it were already telling him a story.

Orpheus nodded approvingly. "A wonderful choice," he said. "Take a seat, make yourself comfortable, and begin reading. I will be nearby."

Greg settled onto a soft, starlit pillow and opened the book, feeling a gentle breeze drift through the library as he turned the first page. The words glowed softly on the page, almost as if they were made of stardust.

As he read, the story unfolded before him, filling his mind with peaceful images. The book told of a quiet forest bathed in moonlight, where the trees whispered gentle songs, and soft patches of moss glowed in the dark. The forest was home to all sorts of calm, friendly creatures—deer with silvery coats, rabbits with soft, fluffy tails, and even fireflies that lit up the night like tiny stars.

As he continued reading, Greg felt himself growing more and more relaxed. The gentle descriptions of the moonlit forest wrapped around him like a warm blanket, and he could almost hear the soft rustling of leaves and the quiet hum of the forest creatures.

Before he knew it, Greg's eyes were growing heavy, and he let out a soft yawn. Sensing his drowsiness, Orpheus appeared beside him, his eyes filled with warmth.

"Come, Greg," Orpheus said gently. "It's time for

you to return home, where the story will continue in your dreams."

Greg nodded sleepily, hugging the book to his chest as he climbed onto Orpheus's back once more. The owl lifted him gently, gliding out of the library and back into the open sky.

As they flew, Greg felt a comforting drowsiness settle over him, and he closed his eyes, holding the memories of the Starlight Library close. He could still feel the warmth of the feather bookmark in his hand, reminding him of the magical library and the dreams that waited within its glowing shelves.

When they reached his window, Orpheus set him gently on his bed, tucking the feather bookmark under his pillow. Greg smiled, feeling a wave of gratitude wash over him as he looked at the wise owl.

"Thank you, Orpheus," he whispered, his voice soft with sleep.

Orpheus gave a gentle nod, his eyes twinkling with kindness. "Goodnight, Greg. Remember, whenever you need a new story, the Starlight Library will be waiting for you."

With one last flap of his wings, Orpheus disappeared into the night, leaving behind a soft, comforting breeze.

Greg lay back on his bed, the feather bookmark

tucked safely under his pillow. As he closed his eyes, he felt the gentle warmth of the Starlight Library filling his heart, and soon, he drifted into a peaceful sleep.

In his dreams, he found himself in the moonlit forest once again, wandering through the soft, glowing trees. The deer and rabbits greeted him with friendly nods, and the fireflies lit up the path, guiding him deeper into the forest. The air was filled with a quiet, soothing hum, and Greg felt completely at ease, surrounded by the gentle glow of starlit pages.

From that night on, Greg knew that the Starlight Library was always there, waiting for him among the stars, ready to share its stories and fill his dreams with magic and wonder.

# Conclusion

As our journey through these sleepy stories comes to an end, it's time to settle down, close your eyes, and drift off into dreams of moonlit forests, magical libraries, and sparkling seas. I hope each story has filled your heart with warmth and wonder, bringing you closer to the cozy world of dreams where imagination knows no bounds.

Remember, whenever you long for another adventure or a comforting tale before bed, these stories will be here, ready to guide you to lands of peace and magic. Dreams are our nighttime journeys, our moments to explore and to rest, and every page of these stories is a gentle step toward those dreams.

If you enjoyed these tales, look for other books by Willow Wiggins, where you'll find even more cozy stories crafted to help you relax, unwind, and journey to magical places with every turn of the page. Each story holds a gentle invitation to explore, to wonder, and to let your imagination carry you on soft, sleepy adventures.

So, close your eyes, take a deep breath, and let sleep wrap around you like a warm blanket. Sweet dreams, dear reader. May tonight's dreams be as cozy and magical as the stories we've shared.

If you liked this book, please check out my other books. Just search for "Willow Wiggins."

And lastly, leaving reviews on my books is a giant help. If you would be kind enough to take 60 seconds to leave a review, I would be forever grateful.

With love and respect,
Willow